Duncan McLellan

Glasgow public parks

Duncan McLellan

Glasgow public parks

ISBN/EAN: 9783743310360

Manufactured in Europe, USA, Canada, Australia, Japa

Cover: Foto ©Lupo / pixelio.de

Manufactured and distributed by brebook publishing software (www.brebook.com)

Duncan McLellan

Glasgow public parks

yours truly
D. McLellan

LASGOW

UBLIC PARKS.

BY

DUNCAN M'LELLAN,
Superintendent of Parks,
1853-1893.

Illustrated by Annan & Sons, Glasgow.

GLASGOW:
JOHN SMITH & SON, 19 RENFIELD STREET.
1894.

PREFACE.

A FEW words are required by way of preface to this Volume.

On the Author's recent retirement, after forty years' service, some of his friends, in view of his long connection with the Public Parks of Glasgow, suggested that he might fittingly occupy some leisure hours in writing a few papers on the subject, and these appeared in the *Glasgow Herald*.

Subsequently it was thought that they might not be unacceptable in collected form. It is with some diffidence that the Author accedes to this request. The employment of his life has been the cultivation of other flowers than those of composition; and the articles in the present volume have no literary pretensions, nor do they profess to be an exhaustive treatment of the subject. They aim at presenting, in a concise way, the main facts as to the origin, progress, and present aspect of our Public Parks, with a few notes regarding their natural history. If they afford information to his readers, or if they serve to foster the interest and the pride of the citizens of Glasgow in their Public Parks, the Author's chief desire in publishing them will be met, and his labour more than compensated.

In conclusion, the Author desires gratefully to acknowledge valuable assistance from his official and other personal friends; and, if he might be permitted to refer to friends of the past, he would mention, with deepest respect, the late Mr. John Carrick, City Architect, whose name is inseparably associated with the Parks of Glasgow and the many schemes of City Improvement during the last fifty years.

D. M'L.

7 KELVINGROVE TERRACE,
  GLASGOW, *December, 1894.*

CONTENTS.

		PAGE
1.	GLASGOW GREEN,	9
2.	KELVINGROVE PARK,	41
3.	QUEEN'S PARK AND CAMPHILL,	71
4.	ALEXANDRA PARK,	86
5.	CATHKIN BRAES,	95
6.	BOTANIC GARDENS,	101
7.	MAXWELL PARK,	114
8.	SPRINGBURN AND RUCHILL PARKS,	119
9.	PUBLIC SQUARES AND OPEN SPACES,	123
10.	THE ELDER PARK, GOVAN,	136
11.	VICTORIA PARK, PARTICK,	144
12.	APPENDICES,	151

ILLUSTRATIONS.

FRONTISPIECE PHOTOGRAVURE.

To face Page

1. GLASGOW GREEN, looking East,   10
2.   Do.,   do.   West,   22
3. KELVINGROVE PARK, looking North,   42
4.   Do.,   Views in,   56
5. QUEEN'S PARK, looking West,   74
6.   Do.,   Views in,   80
7. ALEXANDRA PARK,   86
8. CATHKIN BRAES, -   96
9. BOTANIC GARDENS,   102
10. MAXWELL PARK, -   114
11. CATHEDRAL AND PHŒNIX SQUARES,   130
12. THE ELDER PARK, GOVAN,   136
13. VICTORIA PARK, PARTICK, -   144

GLASGOW PUBLIC PARKS.

I. GLASGOW GREEN.

GLASGOW GREEN, the oldest as well as the largest of the city parks, owes its origin to the common lands of the burgh. About the year 1178 these lands consisted of an irregularly shaped area of ground, which had been gifted by the Crown, by the Church, and by private individuals, and were primarily set apart for the pasturing of cattle, and for the general benefit of the burgesses. They extended as far north as Cowlairs and Springburn; as far west as Hamilton Hill, New City Road, North Woodside Road, Garscube Road, and St. Enoch Square; and were bounded on the south by the Clyde, and on the east by the Camlachie Burn and the Garngad Burn. Up to the beginning of the sixteenth century the above area represented, in a general way, the common lands of the burgh; but about that time the burgh authorities found it necessary, probably owing to financial difficulties, to sell or feu a considerable portion of their property, including some of the lands which are now known as Glasgow Green. In the course of time it was seen that this had been a mistake, and steps were taken to rectify it as far as possible. To effect this object funds were required, and these were obtained by selling other portions of the common lands, from the proceeds of which the present Glasgow Green was acquired. The purchases so made were most judicious. In 1662, the lands of Linningshaugh (Linen Haugh) were acquired; in 1664, Peitboig (Peat Bog) and Dassie (Daisy) Green; from 1664 to 1770, Kilelaith; Milndam from 1665 to 1670; Cropnestock or Craignestock from 1680 to 1688; Milnhill from 1685 to 1690; Broomlands in 1770; and, finally, in 1792, the lands of Provosthaugh, which are now well known to the citizens of Glasgow as the Fleshers' Haugh, were secured as an open space for all time to come. It would be tedious if one were to follow out the history of each of these acquisitions, but at the same time it is worthy of note that the common lands, the real property of the citizens, were in great part alienated from the city, and that the remainder were sold for the purpose of re-acquiring what is now known as Glasgow Green.

From the above sketch it will be seen that Glasgow Green has varied considerably in extent from time to

Glasgow Green, looking east.

time. In 1730, from a plan made out by James Moor, land surveyor, it contained only 59 acres, 1 rood, 10 falls. During the rest of the eighteenth century the size of the Green steadily increased, until, in 1810, it had risen to 117 acres, 1 rood, 29 falls, according to a survey made by Mr. William Kyle, the City Surveyor. Shortly after that date the city acquired power from Parliament to sell certain portions for the public offices and jail, for the street leading to Hutcheson's Bridge, for Monteith Row, &c., so that when these transactions were completed Mr. Kyle made another survey, and found the total acreage to be 108 acres, 2 roods, 17 falls. Since that time some changes have been made, and the total area of the Green is now 136 imperial acres.

When one takes into consideration the original purpose for which the common lands of the ancient Burgh of Glasgow were intended, it is not difficult to find a reason for the laxity which prevailed in the laying out of the common green or park in early times. When a burgh has a property which is common to all the citizens for the grazing of their cattle, and for the less lucrative but not less needful purpose of washing and drying clothes, it is to be expected that little interest will be taken in the ornamentation of such a tract of land; but at the same time we find that something was done in this way at a very early period.

We find that, as far back as 28th March, 1600, "it is
" statute be the provest, balleis, and counsall that the haill
" inhabitants within this town, bothe fre and onfrie, being
" warnit be sound of drum or otherwyis sufficientlie, send
" furth out of ilk hous ane servand to the Greyne to the
" common work of the calsaye" (causeway) "and ytherwyis
" as thei salbe commandit be the balleis and maister of
" work onder the pane of Vj s. 8d. to be payit be ilk
" maister of the hous, and the penalte to be applyit to the
" said work, and the officeris to pas with the maister of
" work and poynd for the same."

The foregoing is the earliest record to be found of any direct effort towards the laying-out of the Green, and it has proved a solid foundation for the interest which the citizens of Glasgow have taken in their public parks, for the jealous spirit with which they have guarded them, and for the generous manner in which they have ungrudgingly contributed towards enlarging their extent and towards their upkeep. Taxation is always a delicate subject to mention, but it is rarely that one hears any exception taken to the amount which the Parks yearly cost the city.

During the seventeenth century the Green was almost entirely devoted to objects of practical use to the community—viz., the grazing of cattle and washing of clothes, both of which will be noticed later on; but in the meantime it may prove of interest, from a landscape point of view, to observe the various developments in the laying out of the park.

In 1647 the burgh ordained "that the Mr of Work to "cause pleughe and harrow the grein in so far as is flaine," (or the turf pared off,) "and to mak it evene and dress "about the stank," (a pool of standing water.) Afterwards, in 1660, a desire was shewn for the planting of more trees, as we find that on 18th February of that year the burgh "recommends to Bailie Campbell and the Deane of Gild "to cause plant some tries about the grein, and to consider "upon the overtour maid be William Cummyng anent the "cutting of ane trie in the Kirk Yaird, and he to plant "twelfe theirfor elsewhere." The latter part of the foregoing extract is interesting, as it points to a decided wish, on the part of the magistrates of that date, to protect the trees of the city,—a characteristic feature which has always been maintained.

Again, on 30th July, 1659, the burgh "recommends to "the Deane of Gild to cause fill up against the cast that "was made in the Meikle Green, and mak that part thereof "level with the rest of the Grein, and agrei with any "persons thereanent who will do it chiepest."

As far as can be definitely ascertained, the Green was originally endowed with a considerable wealth of fine old trees, which, unfortunately, have gradually disappeared under the influence of the smoky atmosphere which has inevitably accompanied the commercial growth of the city. Two trees seem to have been specially favoured in the Green, the elm and the ash,—and in all the records we find mention of avenues of these trees. All traces of them have disappeared, and one must be content to imagine what they were, and to endeavour to replace them by other varieties which will grow and give some life and character to this fine old park.

A source of trouble in the early history of the Green was the constant flooding of the lower parts of it; and this has always received attention from the city authorities. The ground is low-lying, especially towards the bend of the Fleshers' Haugh, and the main object has generally been to fill up rather than to embank. The latter method of overcoming such a difficulty is seldom satisfactory, especially from a landscape point of view, and it must be a matter of congratulation to the citizens of Glasgow that, at the present time, an opportunity has been afforded them, owing to railway operations, of improving upon the Green, even though it is at the expense of its outward characteristics for some time to come.

The general condition of the Green prior to the year 1810, is given in a report published in the year 1828 by

Dr. Cleland, who was at that time Superintendent of Public Works. From this report we gather that the approaches to the Low Green were in an imperfect and inadequate condition, being narrow and inconvenient. There seem also to have been tan-works, slaughter-houses, and other offensive works in close proximity; and the public washing-place was still in its old and objectionable position near to Nelson's Monument. The Calton Green was irregular and swampy, and the banks contiguous to the Peat Bog were rugged. The Provost or Fleshers' Haugh was separated from the High Green and King's Park by a large ditch filled with springs, which made the whole haugh soft and marshy.

The foregoing was therefore the general condition of the Green prior to 1810, and the improvements made by Dr. Cleland, during his tenure of office, can best be given in his own words:—

"In the autumn of 1813, then a member of the Town "Council, I was permitted to make a plan and draw up a "report for improving the Green; which having been ap-"proven of, the plan was engraved and the report printed "at the expense of the Corporation. In the spring of "1815, soon after my appointment to the office of Sup-"erintendent of Public Works, the improvements were "commenced, but it was greatly owing to the pressure

"of the times and the want of work for the labouring
"classes in the years 1816, 1819, and 1826, that the
"improvements were carried on with so much rapidity.
"In these years of general distress subscriptions were
"raised and Relief Committees formed, when weavers
"and others who could not get employment at their
"respective trades were sent to improve the Green."

"During the autumn and the spring of 1817, 146
"weavers were employed in levelling and turfing King's
"Park and forming walks on its boundaries. On the
"2nd August, 1819, 324 weavers (comprising 124 born
"in Glasgow, 96 other places in Scotland, 101 Irish,
"2 English, and 1 American) commenced to slope and
"level the High Green and Calton Green, some parts
"of which required an excavation of not less than 6 feet,
"and others a filling-up of nearly 5 feet. The tunnel
"for the Camlachie and Molendinar Burns was made
"from William Street, near the head of the Green, to
"the Episcopal Chapel, near the foot of Saltmarket.
"In the spring of 1820 rubbish began to be laid down
"in the Low Green, for raising it out of the reach of
"floods. In some places the filling-up was nearly 6 feet.
"In about two years the whole was brought to its present
"level. In 1821 the public washing-house was removed
"to its present site near William Street, and pipes were

"laid for conveying filtered water to the bleaching
"grounds."

In 1826 a very important improvement was commenced, when 164 weavers and other operatives sent by the Relief Committee were employed. This consisted of cutting a deep ditch and constructing a large sewer for carrying off the springs from the south bank of the High Green and King's Park, thus completely draining the Fleshers' Haugh. The banks of the High Green and King's Park were levelled and the open ditches in the Haugh filled up, and during the autumn trees were planted and walks formed.

An interesting feature in the laying-out of the Green, which shewed the lively interest manifested by the citizens in the undertaking, was the fact that, late in the year 1826, a public subscription was raised for the philanthropic object already referred to, of providing work for unemployed weavers and others, and for the formation of a good carriage-way or drive round the Green. This drive was about 2½ miles long, and cost £1070. Of this sum £400 was contributed by the Corporation, and 13 private citizens contributed £20 each, and 41 £10 each. Those who gave £20 had the privilege of using the ride and drive with a four-wheeled carriage, and the £10 subscribers with a one-horse carriage or a riding horse for life. By Act of Parliament passed in 1827, the Council were empowered to complete this carriageway, and also to levy tolls upon all persons using it, except those who were subscribers to the original fund. On 15th May, 1828, the ride or drive was opened. On 10th December, 1830, it was found that the net drawings from persons paying a toll, after deducting the wages of a toll-keeper, were only £95 5s., and the toll was thereupon reduced to one-half of its former rate. On 23rd April, 1857, it was resolved that the tolls upon cabs and carriages for admission to the Green should be abolished.

About this time the Green was formally taken over as a public park, in contradistinction to the common green of the city, which had been really its character previously. The formation of Kelvingrove Park had awakened a growing desire amongst the public to improve the open spaces available for the recreation of the citizens, and to make them more attractive from a landscape point of view. The Council authorized the sum of £315 to be expended in making new walks, in planting trees and shrubs, and in enclosing certain portions with iron railings,—all of which gave the Green a more park-like appearance. Yearly improvements were made in this way, until a complete belting of young trees was planted all round the margin of the Green from Jail Square to Allen's Pen. Clumps of trees of considerable size were also planted in various parts of the Green and along the banks of the Clyde, especially in the vicinity of the springboards and bathing-houses. In 1878 the Glasgow Public Parks Act was passed, and in that year the up-keep of all the parks, including the Green, was defrayed from assessments levied under powers conferred by the Act, thus removing the necessity of applying for special grants for yearly expenditure. Reference has already been made to the employment of weavers and other operatives in times of depression in trade. This scheme has been utilized at various times, notably in 1858, 1878, and 1886, and has proved of considerable benefit in improving and laying out the parks, as well as providing a means of livelihood for large numbers of individuals who would otherwise have been starving.

In 1860 a gymnasium was presented by the late D. G. Fleming of Manchester to his native city, and was erected in the Green on the site on which it at present stands. It has afforded much amusement and healthful recreation to large numbers of boys and young men, and is always largely patronized.

On the banks of the Clyde there were formerly several mineral wells, which possessed special characteristics from their chemical ingredients. One of them, known as Robin's Well, was situated at the bend of the river, and is understood to have been famous for its bleaching qualities; but all trace of it has now disappeared. Another well, which was situated on the brae-face of that part of the Green between the Humane Society House and Nelson's Monument, was known as "Arn's Well"; but it also has disappeared. The name was derived from a group of alder or arn trees which originally grew near to the spring. The water from this well was considered the purest and best in the city, and was in great demand for making specially good tea and punch. It is reported that it was near this spot, when walking on a Sunday afternoon, that the idea of his great improvement on the steam engine first flashed upon the mind of James Watt.

Of recent years various drinking fountains have been erected in the Green. In 1866 the Corporation caused four to be placed in various positions, to take the place of the old spring wells, which were found to have become contaminated and unfit for use. In 1873 Bailie (now Sir James) Bain erected a handsome fountain at the park entrance at the foot of Charlotte Street. In 1878 another one was presented by the friends of Sir William Collins, as an acknowledgment of his services to the temperance cause, and erected at the main entrance to the Green opposite the Court-houses. There is also another drinking fountain which deserves to be noticed. On the 2nd of June, 1881, permission was granted by the Town Council to the club known as the "Ramblers "Round Glasgow," to erect a fountain to the memory of Hugh Macdonald, the author of *Rambles Round Glasgow*, who has done so much to let the citizens know the beauty of the environs of our great city. This fountain was originally placed on Gleniffer Braes, near Paisley, but it suffered considerably from bad usage from the public, and it was accordingly removed to the Green, where it now stands. The Doulton Fountain, which figured so conspicuously at the Glasgow Exhibition of 1888 in Kelvingrove Park, was re-erected by Sir Henry Doulton in the Green upon the broad walk between the Nelson Monument and the Court-houses, and was formally handed over to the city on 29th August, 1890. The ground round it has been laid out with trees, shrubs, and flowers; and during the summer evenings, when the fountain is playing, it forms a source of attraction to many visitors.

Up till the year 1860 little or no money had been expended on the Green in the way of providing a flower garden, but in that year the portion between Monteith

Row and the carriage drive was laid out in flower beds, mainly in the way of an experiment, as it was feared that the smoky atmosphere would seriously interfere with a good display of bloom. Fortunately these fears have not been realized, and year by year the show of flowers has improved. Special attention has been paid to the different varieties which seem to grow best, and there are many foliage plants which appear almost miraculously to thrive upon smoke and soot. The public have always taken a special interest in the flower garden, and it has been mainly owing to their guardianship that the flowers are allowed to flourish and bloom without almost a single one of them being plucked or stolen. The flower garden remained in its original site until 1889, when the operations of the Caledonian Railway Company necessitated its removal. A new site was therefore found lower down, nearer to the centre of the Green; and in that situation it has been very successful. The average number of plants bedded out every year is about 50,000, and there are usually planted about 4,000 bulbs, which make a good display in early spring. The operations of the Railway Company and the unfortunate collapse, in a gale, of Templeton's Mills (happily now restored), caused the removal of the plant-houses, which have been re-erected between London Street and Charlotte Street,

Glasgow Green looking west

and now form a pleasing feature in the Green. The old site has been laid out as a place of shelter with trees, flowers, and shrubs.

Reference has already been made to the use of the Green for grazing purposes, and at one time the revenue realized from this source was of considerable amount. At first it was customary to let out the grazing to a tacksman or tenant, who paid a slump sum per annum for the privilege of pasturing his cattle. In the year 1666 we find from the Burgh Records that the sum of £31 2s. 2d. was realized from this source, and as the extent of the Green gradually increased, this annual revenue steadily rose. The largest amount received, whilst this custom of letting the grass to one person was continued, was in the year 1682, when the annual rent reached the figure of £185 3s. 4d.; and for two consecutive years—1692 and 1693—it was £177 15s. 6d. After that time the rents appear to have decreased, probably owing to the fact that larger numbers of the public were frequenting the Green, and in this way interfering with the grazing, so that in 1732 the rent received by the city only amounted to £95 17s. 9d. In 1733 the Council took the matter into consideration, and resolved that for the future the grazing on the Green should be let out to the inhabitants at a fixed rate for each animal, the charge per head being 20 merks Scots money; and that a herd should be appointed to direct and look after the grazing of the cattle. From this source the sum of £67 1s. 9d. was realized in 1733, and in 1734 £89 10s. In the beginning of 1737 the charge per head was £1 for cows and £1 10s. for horses, the number of cows being restricted to 80. This system of letting the grazing was continued down to 1751, the rents varying considerably during that period. The largest sum received in one year was in 1746, when it reached a total of £101 6s. 6d. Since that time the grazings have been let by public roup, and in some years very large sums were received. In 1800 the rents were £249 0s. 6d., and in 1810 a sum of £399 4s. 6d. was received. In a report by Dr. Cleland, in 1813, he mentions that the average number of cows for the previous three years which had paid a grass fee of £3 3s. was 127, or a total sum of £400 1s.; and from the burgh records that sum appears to be the largest ever received in one year for grazing. In 1816 the grass mail was raised to £4 4s., and by the year 1830 the rental had fallen to £228 14s. Thereafter it steadily decreased until 1870, when the grazing of cows ceased on the Green. Since that time various enclosures have been railed in and let for the pasturage of sheep, the average rental from this source for the last four years being £42 10s.

In connection with the grazing on the Green an amusing circumstance is related which occurred towards the end of last century, and which shewed that the citizens were opposed to the use of the Green for any other purpose than public benefit. At that time there was a public crier or bellman, called Bell Geordie, who was quite a character in his way, and who was employed by the citizens to make proclamations. From a newspaper we find that, on 1st May, 1797, he made the following whimsical announcement, which probably originated with himself:—

"Petition of the cows on the Green of Glasgow.—At
"a meeting of the cows of the Green of Glasgow in
"common pasture assembled—the Bull in the chair
"(Bell Geordie was constituted the clerk of the meeting)
"—the following draft of a petition was drawn up and
"unanimously adopted, and ordered to be presented by
"the Town Herd to Queen Charlotte, the *spousa cara*
"of His Britannic Majesty King George the Third,
"protesting to His Majesty against the continual parad-
"ing of Volunteers on one of the best grass plots in
"Scotland that has not been ploughed up since the
"glorious Revolution, a lapse of time during which three

"millions of Glasgow have been born or died on a "moderate computation."

It is to be feared that Bell Geordie's proclamation did not carry much weight with it, but it pointed towards a feeling that large public meetings or gatherings should not be held on the Green.

As might be expected, the Green has always been a favourite place for games and sports of all kinds. From an early time golf was a favourite, and on 27th March, 1792, the Golf Club applied to the Council for leave to "remove the present herd's house or golf-house "in the Green, and to build a new house at their own "expense," which shewed that the club must have been in existence some time previously. The Council, on 1st October of the same year, consented to the erection of a club-house, not to exceed in cost £250, the club paying a rent to the Council and getting a lease for fifteen years, with a break in favour of the city at the end of ten years. How long this club survived cannot be ascertained, but, doubtless, it was the forerunner of the Glasgow Golf Club, which has now its quarters in the Alexandra Park.

As far back as 3rd April, 1675, we find an interesting note about "foot raices," which is taken from the Burgh Records, and is as follows :—

"The said appoynts ane proclamation to be sent "through the town xx for rouping of the greines; as "also a proclamation to be sent throw that ther is a "foot raice to be run thrys about the New Grein on "the xxii of this instant, that who desyres to run may "be admitted and that he who wines sall have twentie "shilling starling."

It does not appear from the records how long the worthy Councillors of that ancient time kept up the custom of encouraging athletic sports amongst the citizens, but probably this generosity would be on the occasion of some public holiday. It would rather surprise the Council of the present day if this precedent were founded on, and if they were asked to vote a sum of money for prizes for "foot raices" in Glasgow Green.

A subject connected with the Green which has attracted public attention on several occasions, is the working of the coal and other minerals under it. Various reports have, from time to time, been obtained from professional gentlemen regarding them, but no definite action has been taken in the matter. In 1821 the Council authorized the expenditure of £150 for boring operations; and, in 1822 and 1824, reports were presented by Dr. Cleland, the superintendent of public works, in which he mentioned that Messrs. Dixon were willing to work the minerals from a pit on the south side of the river. These reports were remitted to a committee, but the matter appears to have been lost sight of. In 1828 the Corporation received a report from Mr. William Dixon of the Govan Colliery, but nothing further was done till 1834, when a committee recommended that the working of the coal was expedient. This committee were authorized to take steps towards the letting of the coal, but the matter was again shelved till 1836, when it was determined to obtain further information regarding the practicability of the proposal, and to get a further report from Mr. Dixon. The previous reports were also ordered to be printed. Towards the end of 1836, Messrs. Ferguson & Son, mineral surveyors, and Mr. John Craig, mineral surveyor, submitted reports, which, along with a report by a committee, were presented to the Council. Nothing further was done till 20th August, 1857, when it was remitted to the Finance Committee to consider the expediency of working the coal. That committee, on 13th January, 1858, recommended that the coal should be exposed to public auction; and, their report having been considered at various meetings, the Corporation gave the committee authority to proceed, the upset price to be a fixed rent of £1,000, and 1s. per twenty cwt. of lordship. When this decision was made public the inhabitants of the eastern part of the city feared that the amenity of the Green might be injured, and at a public meeting resolved to oppose the proposal. This threat caused the matter once more to be delayed; but, on 5th March, 1869, a committee was again appointed to report on the whole subject. A report was obtained from Mr. Ronald Johnstone, C.E., which was to the effect that there was no danger of any injury to the Green by the working of the coals; and he also stated that there were valuable seams of fire-clay, which could be worked along with the coal. A report in these terms was submitted on 14th October, 1869; but consideration of it was delayed, and once more the matter fell into abeyance. Nothing further was done till 5th July, 1888, when a motion was submitted to appoint another committee, but after discussion it was withdrawn. If, as really seems to be the case, there are valuable minerals under the Green, and if they can be worked without much inconvenience to the general public, it certainly would be advantageous to utilize some of the wealth, at present lying dormant, for the general benefit of the city.

A notable feature in connection with the use of the Green by the public was the "Shows," as they were called, which were held on the western portion of the park for many years during the week of Glasgow Fair.

As was to be expected, the Common Green of the city proved the most suitable spot on which to hold such exhibitions, and the annual saturnalia of the holiday season attracted vast numbers of the travelling shows and caravans, which, even more than in the present time, went the round of the country. For a considerable period they were allowed the use of the Green free of any charge, but their numbers became so great, and the space they occupied so large, that the Council had to take the matter in hand. Accordingly, in 1815, it was resolved to charge a rent, and in that year the moneys exacted from parties holding shows amounted to £104 3s. 6d., and the total for the eight years up to 1822, was £690 14s. In the latter year the shows and entertainments were classified as follows:—Wild beasts, 2; giantess, 1; giants, 2; tumbling, &c., 6; fat bull, 1; waxwork, &c., 1; a beast, 1; roundabouts, 6; sundry entertainments, 5. These shows continued to be held on the Green till 1871, and the rents received from them amounted to a large sum. In 1830 there was received £122 16s. 3d.; in 1840, £246; in 1850, £374 4s. 6d.; in 1860, £397 17s. 11d.; in 1870, £590 3s. 10d.; and in 1871, £45 4s. 6d. The total amount received in fifty-three years—1819-71—was £14,828 10s., being an average of £280 yearly.

The most of the buildings in connection with these shows were of a temporary description, but the proprietors of several of the larger entertainments obtained leases of longer duration than a year, and erected buildings of a more substantial character. In 1845, however, the Council, on the petition of 60,000 inhabitants, ordered these erections to be cleared away. In 1866 an application by Mr. Hengler for permission to erect a circus for six months was refused; and, on 2nd February, 1870, the Council resolved that the shows should only be allowed on the Green for two weeks during the New-Year holidays, and for three weeks at the Fair time. This practically put an end to the holding of shows on the Green, and none were held there after the following year, 1871. The space occupied in that year extended fully two-thirds of the way towards the Nelson Monument from the Court-houses, so that when the glories of Glasgow Fair were at their height the area taken up by them must have been of very large extent. Since their removal from the Green the shows have had to shift their quarters more than once. But they are yearly diminishing in numbers and in popularity, and it may with certainty be predicted, that before long they will be a thing of the past.

Before the city of Glasgow possessed its present abundant water supply, the public Green was used by the citizens as the place for washing and bleaching clothes. This custom was, and still is, common in almost all rural villages which have a common green; and for many years the citizens of Glasgow had no other means at their disposal for such a necessary purpose. The water of the Clyde was then pure, and well adapted for washing linen. This fact, coupled with the abundance of the supply, and the facilities afforded for bleaching upon the extensive grass swards, caused many of the housewives of Glasgow to frequent it. The authorities, therefore, were compelled to offer facilities for such a good purpose, and they accordingly erected a public washing-house. The date of its erection is somewhat uncertain, but it was in existence about the year 1741. There was a well in the centre of the bleaching green, which is marked upon an old plan. Upon the same plan there is a building called "Castle Boins," which is close to the Camlachie Burn, and a little to the east of the site of the English Chapel. This building seems to have got the name of "Castle Boins" from the number of boynes or tubs which would be in its vicinity on a fine washing day; and, from its proximity to the Camlachie Burn, it shews that the water of that stream, then clear and limpid, was extensively used by the washerwomen.

At that time the washing was performed in the usual way of a Scotch washing—viz., by treading or tramping on the clothes; but, by an edict of the Magistrates, dated 11th October, 1623, this was prohibited in public, under a penalty of eleven shillings Scots for each offence, and was only allowed "in housis and private placis." The old "Castle Boins" appears, some time afterwards, to have become a house of refreshment, or ale-house, much resorted to by the citizens. With regard to the washing-house proper, there was, in 1730, a building supplied with water by a lead or watercourse from the Camlachie Burn; but this does not apply to "Castle "Boins," the north front of which was immediately towards the burn and had direct access to it. The original washing-house was altered and enlarged on various occasions, and in 1807 it was nearly doubled. This washing-house was a source of considerable revenue to the city, but the actual amount is not easily traced. Chapman, in his book on Glasgow, says that "it has been let for "£600 per annum, but since the introduction of water "by pipes into the town, the rent has been much reduced. "It is let from 1811 to 1812 at £284." This decrease in revenue is accounted for by the fact, that a good supply of water was then obtainable at most of the houses in the city,—the Glasgow Water-works and the Cranstonhill

Water-works having been opened in 1806 and 1808. The charges for the use of the washing-house were collected at the Clerks' Lodge, which was situated at the east end of Greendyke Street. The dues leviable by the tacksman or tenant of the washing-house were as follows:—

For hot and cold water of one day's washing, without the use of tubs and stools,	4d.
For the use of a washing tub and washing stool for one day,	1½d.
Watching through the night a day's washing of clothes,	3d.
Boiling clothes in a large boiler,	8d.
Three pailfuls of warm water for rinsing,	1d.

It was, of course, permissible for any one, without charge, to bleach clothes on the Green which had been washed at home, or to warm water in pots for use in washing, or to wash clothes at the banks of the river; but any one using the public washing-house had to pay the above charges to the tacksman. In 1821 the old washing-house was removed to a site near to the foot of William Street, and for many years continued to be frequented by large numbers; but, owing to improvements made in the interiors of dwelling-houses, it was only retained as a matter of convenience for those residing in the immediate vicinity. Between 1870 and 1880 the Corporation authorities, as part of the city improvement scheme, began to take a practical interest in the sanitary arrangements of the city. Accordingly, in 1878, the site of the old washing-house was leased to the Baths Committee at a yearly rent of £67 10s., who erected upon it the present handsome range of buildings, which are equipped not only with all the most thorough appliances for washing clothes, but are also furnished with a complete and elegant system of public baths.

The River Clyde, in so far as the portion of it which passes through the Green is concerned, has not altered so much in its general characteristics as have the lower reaches; and if the now sadly polluted water could only be changed to the limpid stream of former days, it would still possess many of its old attractions and associations. Formerly there were one or two islands in it, the principal one being known as Point Isle; but all traces of it have now disappeared. It was nearly opposite the old well, a short distance below the Humane Society's House; and at that spot the river is still comparatively shallow. There was also another island, called Dovecot Island, farther down the river, below the present Albert Bridge; but it also has been swept away, probably owing to the dredging operations in connection with the deepening of the river. Since 1879 the bed of the

Clyde in the Green has altered considerably, owing to the removal of the weir at the point where the river leaves the Green. Considerable attention has, however, been paid to the banks of the river, which have been pitched, so as to prevent the water undermining the soil. The first pitching operations were commenced in 1843, and since then considerable sums of money have been spent from time to time on this object. When the river was pure and clean the fishing must have been very good, the whole river being famous for its salmon, as the city arms testify; and, doubtless, many good catches of fish were obtained from the banks of the Common Green. There seems also to have been good fishing on the Camlachie and Molindinar Burns, which have now, fortunately in one sense, disappeared from public view.

Bathing in the river was a great attraction for many of the Glasgow citizens, and it is only within recent years that it has been discontinued. The Corporation erected bathing boxes and springboards for the use of the bathers above the bend on the Fleshers' Haugh; but these were removed in 1877, and since that time there has been no bathing in the river. For many years there was a swimming competition in the Clyde on New-Year's Day, but that old custom has also become a thing of the past. As was to be expected, drowning accidents were not uncommon during the summer months; and to obviate, as far as possible, a fatal termination to such occurrences the Humane Society House was founded in 1790. The money necessary for its erection was raised by public subscription, and since then it has been the means of saving many lives. Mr. George Geddes was principal officer for the long period of thirty-two years, prior to his death in 1889. During that time he rescued no fewer than 98 persons from a watery grave. His son George now fills the situation, with credit to himself and his late father. Boating on the river has always attracted many of the rising generation; but the removal of the weir, and, in hot weather, the unpleasant odour from the water, has diminished the popularity of this form of amusement. Regattas, however, are still held during the summer months, and excite a considerable amount of public interest; but it cannot be said that the Clyde, so far as the Green is concerned, possesses many attractions as a rowing course, unless for an enthusiast.

Although a considerable stretch of the river passes through the park, it is worthy of note that there is only one bridge which is actually in the Green—viz., the Suspension Bridge at the Humane Society's House, which was erected in 1853, at a cost of about £6,000. This bridge, however, is only for pedestrians; and there is a decided want of another bridge, to accommodate vehicular traffic, there being no connecting link, except the Suspension Bridge, between the north and the south banks of the river between Rutherglen Bridge and the Albert Bridge. It would be most desirable, therefore, to have some cross connection between the two sides of the river at some point to the east of the present Suspension Bridge.

There is one important landmark in the Green which deserves to be noticed. In 1806 the citizens of Glasgow raised, by public subscription, a monument to the memory of Lord Nelson; and it took the form of a freestone obelisk, which was erected on the Green. It stands about 144 feet high, and is a very handsome column. It was, unfortunately, struck by lightning in 1810; and although the damage was soon repaired, traces of the occurrence are still visible.

One of the few old customs of the Green still remains almost as vigorous as of old, and it is one with which most Glasgow citizens are not very well acquainted, at least those of them who do not reside in its immediate vicinity. From time immemorial it has been the custom for all classes of preachers and debaters to air their eloquence upon the masses who frequent the Green; and on fine Saturday and Sunday afternoons numerous knots of people are to be found listening to discussions upon all varieties of topics. In many cases eccentricity and a certain desire for notoriety are the chief impulses which move the speakers; but at the same time the listener must be often struck with the evident earnestness of the orators, whose eloquence is generally more spontaneous and forcible than polished and refined. Religion, in all its phases, is the most common topic of discussion; but the subjects are many and varied.

As is to be expected, the number of people taking advantage of the Green is very large, and on a recent fine Sunday in August, 78,420 persons were counted as they entered by the gates. The musical performances during the summer months are also largely patronized. The season extends from the beginning of June to the end of August, and the attendance usually averages about 7,000.

With regard to the flora and fauna of the Green, there is, unfortunately, not very much to be said. The constant tramping of the sward has almost entirely caused any indigenous plants to disappear, and year by year this is growing worse. Forty years ago Hugh Macdonald, in his *Rambles Round Glasgow*, mentions that a considerable variety of wild plants could then be found growing within the precincts of the Green, and that probably sixty species could be gathered by a diligent botanist. This, however, is no longer the case, as will be evident to the most casual observer.

As will be seen from the subjoined list, there are a considerable number of birds which still frequent the Green, notwithstanding its smoky atmosphere. They form a most interesting study, and it is to be hoped that their numbers will not diminish.

1. Song Thrush, *Turdus musicus*, L.—Occasionally seen.
2. Fieldfare, *Turdus pilaris*, L.—Seldom seen, and only as a winter visitor.
3. Blackbird, *Turdus merula*, L.—Often seen.
4. Redbreast, *Frithacus rubecula*, L.—Seen in winter.
5. Blue Titmouse, *Parus cæruleus*, L.—Numerous.
6. Pied Wagtail, *Motacilla lugubris*, Semminck.—Common.
7. Grey Wagtail, *Motacilla sulphuræ*, Bechstein.—Common.
8. Yellow Wagtail, *Motacilla raii*, Bonaparte.—Common.
9. Skylark, *Alauda arvensis*, L.—Heard singing occasionally; and visits the Green in flocks during winter.
10. Snow Bunting, *Plectrophanes nivalis*, L.—A winter visitor; sometimes in large flocks.
11. Yellow Bunting, *Emberiza citrinella*, L.—Frequent.
12. Chaffinch, *Fringilla calebs*, L.—Common.
13. House Sparrow, *Passer domesticus*, L.—Abundant.
14. Greenfinch, *Coccothraustes chloris*, L.—Common, and nests.
15. Starling, *Sturnus vulgaris*, L.—Common.
16. Rook, *Corvus frugilegus*, L.—Frequent.
17. Swallow, *Hirundo rustica*, L.—Common.
18. Black-headed Gull, *Larus ridibundus*, L.—Common.
19. Mallard or Wild Duck, *Anes Boscas*, L.—Occasionally seen.

II.

KELVINGROVE PARK.

KELVINGROVE PARK is the first example of the Glasgow Town Council purchasing a large area of ground for the recreation and amusement of the citizens. It was about the year 1852 that the scheme was first started; and, whilst there were many liberal-minded men who gave their aid in carrying out the idea, it is generally acknowledged that the late James Scott of Kelly was the leading spirit in the acquisition of the lands of Kelvingrove.

The lands first purchased were Kelvingrove, from Colin M'Naughton's Trustees, and Woodlands, from the Edinburgh and Glasgow Railway Company, both in the year 1852. In addition, the Corporation acquired portions of several adjoining properties belonging to the Trustees of John Fleming of Clairmont, James M'Hardy, Archibald Campbell of Blythswood, and David Smith. The total area was about 66 acres, and the price paid was £77,945, making the average price per square yard about 4s. 11d. These 66 acres were expressly declared to be for the purposes of a public park, and were not to be built upon or sold; but the Council retained the power of building upon the southern part of Kelvingrove for a width of 120 feet in front of Royal Terrace and Park Grove Terrace,—a right which still remains in their hands. They also set apart for feuing purposes the crest of the hill, which is now known as Park Terrace, Park Gardens, Park Circus, and Park Quadrant,—all ornamental self-contained residences. Under the terms of the titles granted to the purchasers of the feus, it was provided, that for all time coming the remaining portions of the lands should be used only as a public park; but the Corporation reserved the right to erect a winter garden,—a suggestion made by Sir Joseph Paxton in his original design for the laying-out of the park. The laying-out of the grounds was commenced in 1853, and was carried out upon the lines of the plan submitted by him.

Those parts of the lands of Gilmorehill, Clayslaps, and Kelvinbank, which now form part of the park, were not contemplated in the original scheme, and have been added to it in consequence of the erection of the University and the Western Infirmary. The Parks Committee, in acquiring these lands, took a considerable amount of

Wilmington Park looking north

time and trouble to accomplish what they had in view. The late Mr. John Carrick, the Master of Works, in a report by him in 1884, states:—

"Numerous minutes tell of efforts in that direction, "but the difficulty of arranging with the Trades' House, "who were then proprietors of Kelvinbank, prevented "the attainment of this object, and so matters remained "until the railway legislation of 1864 authorized the "Glasgow and South-Western and North British Railway "Companies to acquire the old College in High Street. "The Senatus of the University, who, meanwhile, had "again endeavoured to arrange with the Town Council "for a site on the lands of Woodlands, lost no time in "securing the properties known as Gilmorehill and "Donaldshill; and the subject of park extension was in "this way brought under the consideration of the Town "Council, who, by the provisions of the Glasgow Public "Parks Act of 1859, were authorized to levy an assess- "ment of twopence per pound, and to borrow, in addition "to the sums then owing to the Corporation, a further "sum of £30,000 for the purposes of the said Act. "After protracted negotiations between the Town Council "and the University Authorities, a scheme of arrange- "ment was arrived at on the following basis:—The "Senatus was to retain, for University purposes, the site

"which the University now occupies. The Town Council,
"as Parks Trustees, were to contribute £19,000 for 20½
"acres of ground to extend the Kelvingrove Park, and
"the Corporation were to assume the remaining lands
"of Donaldshill, to be disposed of by them as they
"should think fit. By a subsequent contract of excam-
"bion, the Corporation trransferred nearly the whole of
"these lands to the University in exchange for the lands
"of Clayslaps, which had been purchased as a site for
"a hospital; and the Western Infirmary was thereafter
"erected on Donaldshill."

The additions made to the park in terms of the above arrangement, therefore, consisted of Clayslaps, together with the site of the old mills, a part of Overnewton (acquired from the City Improvement Trustees), Kelvinbank (acquired from the Trades' House), and a small area of ground purchased from the Incorporation of Bakers. The rates paid for the several properties varied from 9s. per square yard for Clayslaps to 45s. per square yard for the site of the mills, the average price being 12s. 2d. per square yard. The price paid for the extent of Gilmorehill, acquired under arrangement with the University, was 3s. 9d. per square yard.

Kelvingrove House was built by Mr. Patrick Colquhoun in 1782. The grounds extended to about 12 acres, and were enclosed by a wall, and laid out as pleasure grounds, with extensive gardens and other accessories to a gentleman's country house. Kelvingrove was more than one mile from the most westmost part of the city, and was justly considered one of the most beautiful country residences around Glasgow, its natural beauty being celebrated in the well-known song by Dr. Lyle, "Let "us haste to Kelvingrove." Mr. Colquhoun, who was thus the founder of Kelvingrove, was a native of Dumbartonshire, and related to the Colquhouns of Luss. He was one of the leading merchants of Glasgow, and Lord Provost of the city in the year 1772. Several years after building Kelvingrove he took up his residence permanently in London, and in 1792 he sold the estate to Mr. John Pattison, who added some 12 acres to the property, which he acquired from the Blythswood Trustees, thereby increasing its extent to some 24 acres in all. Mr. Pattison resided at Kelvingrove for some years, and eventually sold it, in 1806, to Mr. R. Dennistoun. It remained in his family till 1841, when it was conveyed by his sons to Mr. Colin M'Naughton, and finally acquired by the city from his Trustees in the year 1853.

The old mansion-house of Gilmorehill formed, for many years prior to the erection of the University, a conspicuous and attractive object in the landscape, its position being almost exactly in the centre of the present College quadrangle. It was built in 1802 by Robert Bogle, Junior. The lands adjoining the mansion-house extended to about 60 acres, and were purchased from several proprietors during the years 1800-1803. A portion of the grounds was laid out in walks and ornamental shrubberies, whilst a large walled garden contained an extensive range of greenhouses, vineries, &c. There was also connected with the house a lodge, situated on the Partick road, and very commodious stables, ice-house, &c. When at its best Gilmorehill must have been a very beautiful residence, commanding a magnificent and extensive view of all the surrounding country. Mr. Bogle made it his residence until his death in 1822, when he was succeeded by his eldest son, Archibald, who retained possession of it until the year 1845,—memorable for the formation of many joint-stock companies,—when he sold it to one of these undertakings for a large sum, the purpose being the formation of a rural cemetery. The scheme was never successful, and finally the whole estate was sold to the University of Glasgow in the year 1865.

The turning of the first sod to prepare the ground for the erection of the University was performed by Professor Allen Thomson, as chairman of the Building

Committee, on 2nd June, 1866; building operations were commenced in March, 1867; and, when considerable progress had been made, the foundation stone was laid, below the entrance to the Great Hall, on 8th October, 1868, by the Prince and Princess of Wales. The buildings were completed, and the University was opened in November, 1870.

The contrast between the value of these lands, when they were acquired by Mr. Bogle, and the price paid for them by the University, is remarkable. In 1800 Mr. Bogle paid £8,500 for them, and in 1865 the University had to pay the sum of £81,000 for the land, without any buildings except the mansion-house of Gilmorehill. What their present value would have been, if they had been feued, is difficult to conjecture; but the figures given show that the price paid for them, after an interval of sixty-five years, was nearly ten times their original cost.

The Clayslap Mills, which were situated below what is called the Horse-Shoe Fall, were erected in 1654. Tradition states that they were originally a snuff mill, but the property was acquired by the Incorporation of Bakers in 1771, who added considerably to the buildings, and introduced steam to assist the water-power. The mills continued in full operation till 1874, when the whole property was acquired by the city authorities, who, having demolished the buildings, added the ground to the Park. There are now in the possession of ex-Lord Provost Ure at Cairndhu, Helensburgh, eighteen memorial tablets which were erected on the occasion of the various additions and improvements at the mills. The tablets recorded not only the year of the Christian era, but, in the manner of the old Romans with their Consuls, recorded the names of the Deacon and Collector in office at the time.

Immediately to the south of Kelvingrove House lay the lands of Kelvinbank, consisting of about 12 acres. The house was a quaint old building, surrounded by some fine trees, and was purchased for £1,000, in 1792, by Mr. Wilson, uncle of Mr. Rae Wilson, the Syrian traveller, who ultimately came into possession of it. He sold the property to the Trades' House of Glasgow for £20,000, and they have since re-sold it for £80,000. A considerable portion of the estate, about six acres, now forms part of the Park,—the rest of the property having been sold for feuing purposes.

Woodlands House, built towards the end of the last, or the beginning of the present century, by James M'Nayr, LL.D., the first editor of the *Glasgow Herald*, was situated near to where Park Circus now stands. The lodge was in Woodlands Road, close to the site of Woodlands U. P. Church, and there was a winding avenue of fine old trees up to the house. It latterly became the property, and was long the residence, of Mr. James Buchanan, of James Finlay & Co. In olden times the lands were well covered with copsewood, principally oak, remains of which are still to be seen in what is now called the Oak Walk, immediately below the flagstaff and the Russian guns,—the latter of which were captured at Sebastopol in 1855, and presented by the Government to the city in 1857.

Amongst other objects of interest in Kelvingrove Park is the granite stair, situated near to Park Gardens. It is a very substantial and handsome structure, and was erected, in 1854, at a cost of £10,000. Unfortunately it has been placed in a corner of the Park where it is seldom seen, and not often used by the public. If it had been erected more to the north, and nearer to the centre of the slope from Park Terrace, it would have shown to greater advantage, and would have been an ornament to the Park, as well as of great service to the public.

The Stewart Memorial Fountain, designed by Mr. James Sellars, I.A., was erected by the Water Commissioners, in 1872, to commemorate the introduction of Loch Katrine Water into the City, the formal ceremony having been performed by the Queen, at the entrance to the tunnel on Loch Katrine, on the 14th of October,

1859. Mr. Robert Stewart of Murdostoun, after whom the fountain has been named, was Lord Provost of the city in 1854, when the Act of Parliament was passed giving the city power to bring in the Loch Katrine water; and it was almost entirely owing to Mr. Stewart's exertions, in the face of the greatest opposition, that the bill which has proved such a boon to the city was passed.

A little to the north of the Stewart Fountain is a bronze group representing a tigress and her cubs, designed by Rosa Bonheur, which was presented to his native city by W. S. Kennedy of New York at a cost of £1000. A duplicate of this group stands in the Central Park of New York.

The wooden bridge, now removed, which formerly spanned the Kelvin, deserves a passing notice. It was erected in 1868, and was originally intended for the temporary purpose of accommodating the Prince and Princess of Wales when on their way to lay the foundation stone of the University. Since that time, however, it has proved of great benefit as a connecting link between the portions of the Park on the different sides of the Kelvin. It was built by Mr. Thomas Lamb in the short space of eight days, and has stood the tear and wear of twenty-five years. A new and more substantial structure is now in course of construction on the same site.

There is also a strong iron girder bridge lower down the river, on the direct line of the road between University Avenue and Radnor Street, the foundation stone of which was laid by Sir William Collins on 2nd October, 1880. The old Dumbarton Road bridge has also been utilized for connecting the two sides of the park at Dumbarton Road; and, in addition to being quaint and picturesque in its way, it is a good solid structure, which should stand the river floods for many years to come.

One of the most interesting features in the park is the Museum in the old Kelvingrove House, and a few remarks as to its origin may not be out of place. It was occupied by the superintendent of parks from 1854 to 1864, when the Town Council resolved, for various reasons, to reduce it in size and alter it in appearance very considerably. The plans were prepared and operations were about to be commenced, when the late Bailie Fowler, who was one of the Parks Committee, on looking at the house, remarked that it was a piece of Vandalism to cut and carve upon such a fine old mansion, and that it should either be pulled down altogether, or left as it stood and converted into a museum. When Bailie Fowler's idea was mentioned to the Parks Committee they at once rescinded their former resolution, and took steps to follow out his suggestion as to a museum; and the old house, as it stands, is very little altered since 1864. The late Mr. James Thomson, the first curator, was an enthusiast in Natural History—especially ornithology—and in a very short time the rooms were filled with an interesting collection, which attracted large crowds of people. Ex-Bailie M'Bean, who was convener of the parks in 1876, and took a special interest in the Museum, formed the idea of adding a wing to the old house for industrial subjects. He therefore solicited subscriptions, and in a short time raised the necessary sum. Lord Provost Bain laid the foundation stone of the new wing on 19th December, 1874, and it was formally opened to the public on 18th April, 1876. Over the two principal entrances are busts of the two largest subscribers, Alexander Whitelaw of Gartsherrie, and James White of Overtoun. As a proof of the public interest taken in the Kelvingrove Museum, it is sufficient to say that it is visited by a quarter of a million persons yearly. Such is the origin of museums connected with the city of Glasgow.

At the beginning of the present century the woods of Kelvingrove, Woodlands, and Gilmorehill, were rich in native trees, and each successive proprietor improved them considerably by judicious planting. Amongst other trees of note in the park there was, in 1854, a group of six Canadian poplars upon a circular mound, near to

Kelvingrove House, where the new wing of the Museum now stands. They were about 90 feet high and 1 foot 6 inches in diameter, with clean straight stems for 30 feet, covered with ivy. At that time several were dead, and the others fast decaying. They were called "the "Pattisons," and tradition says that the late John Pattison planted them to commemorate the births of the successive members of his family. Several of the trees were blown down during a severe gale in 1866, and, as those remaining were becoming dangerous, they were all removed soon afterwards.

There is a remarkably fine specimen (one of the finest in the country) of the wych or weeping elm (*Ulmus montana pendula*) upon a mound near to the tigress statue and the Stewart Fountain. This tree was presented to the park by the late Mr. Charles Hamilton, and was transplanted from the old Botanic Gardens in Fitzroy Place, in the year 1856, at a cost of £30. At the junction of the walk past the carpet beds and the carriage drive there is, in excellent health, a good specimen of a mulberry bush (*Morus nigra*), which must be at least 100 years old. In 1854 there were three grand, venerable, old Huntingdon willows near to the entrance at Kelvingrove Street. Two of them have succumbed to old age, but the third still remains standing.

In 1853, in the gardens attached to Kelvingrove House, which occupied the present site of the Stewart Fountain and surrounding flower plots, there stood two specimens of the Chinese Arbor Vitæ (*Thuja Chinensis*), pronounced by the late Sir Joseph Paxton, when visiting the park, to be the finest he had seen in Scotland. After the garden wall was removed they were blown down, during a severe gale, in 1856, and although set up again they never thrived.

A very interesting fact connected with the cutting of names upon the bark of trees is to be seen upon the first beech tree west of the Kelvingrove entrance. John H. Pattison cut his name upon the trunk in 1799, and both name and date are quite legible to the present day. The letters, however, have become very much broader, but not any longer, thus proving that a tree grows from the top and does not elongate from the stem, which has more than once been a disputed point among arboriculturists.

The chestnut, lime, beech, and plane are gradually dying out all over the park, but are being replaced by the poplar, willow, ash, and service trees, which seem to withstand the smoke fairly well and grow quickly.

Whilst the plants native to the park are rapidly disappearing, partly owing to the changed atmosphere, and partly owing to the operations of the gardener, especially with the scythe, there are still a good number to be found, as will be seen from the following list :—

Dandelion, *Leontodon taraxacum.*
Dock, *Rumex crispus.*
Sheep's Sorrel, *Rumex acetosella.*
Plaintain, *Plantago media.*
Ribwort Plaintain, *P. lanceolata.*
Buttercup or Crowfoot, *Ranunculus repens.*
Bedstraw, *Galium saxatile.*
Meadow Soft Grass, *Holcus lanatus.*
Creeping Soft Grass, *H. mollis.*
Coltsfoot, *Tussilago farfara.*
Annual Meadow Grass, *Poa annua.*
Smooth-stalked Grass, *P. pratensis.*
Roughish Grass, *P. Trivialis.*
Blue Bell or Wild Hyacinth, *Hyacinthus non-scriptus.*
Yarrow or Milfoil, *Achillea millefolium.*
Lady's Mantle, *Alchemilla vulgaris.*
Daisy, *Bellis perennis.*
Tormentil, *Tormentilla reptans.*
Broom, *Cytisus scoparius.*
Whin, *Ulex Europæus.*
Wood Hawkweed, *Hieracium sylvaticum.*
Hawthorn, *Cratægus oxyacantha.*
Ragwort, *Senecio Jacobaa.*
Groundsel, *S. vulgaris.*
Bittercress, *Cardamine pratensis.*
Chickweed, *Stellaria media.*
Earthnut, *Bunium flexuosum.*
Bugle, *Ajuga reptans.*
Burdock, *Arctium bardana.*
Sow Thistle, *Sonchus arvensis.*
Cock's-foot Grass, *Dactylis glomerata.*
Speedwell, *Veronica chamaedrys.*

Ox-eye Daisy, *Chrysanthemum leucanthemum.*
Sheep's Fescue Grass, *Festuca ovina.*
Scorpion Grass, *Myosotis arvensis.*
Hairy Wood-rush, *Luzula sylvatica.*
Field Wood-rush, *L. campestris.*
Three varieties of Thistles.

The total area of Kelvingrove Park at the present time is 73¼ acres, but, from the natural and undulating character of the ground, it appears to be nearly double that size. The University, with its elevated and artistic outline and its extensive grounds sloping towards the Kelvin, is only separated from the park by a slight iron railing, and appears as part of it. The natural beauty of the scenery of Kelvingrove must have been very fine in the early part of the century, and there are still many traces of it to be found. In particular, the view up the river from the old Kelvin Bridge is very pretty, especially in early spring, when the foliage is fresh and green. Both banks of the river are clothed with partly natural wood, and there still remain goodly clumps of the broom, the whin, and the hawthorn growing indigenous to the soil. The effect of this view is very much enhanced when the river is in flood, both the lower and the upper falls having a most picturesque appearance.

Near to the lower fall, on the north side of the river, there has been in existence, for a great many years, a

Kelvingrove Park. River Kelvin.

Kelvingrove Park. View of the Lake.

mineral well. It was brought prominently before the public by Mr. Napier, a chemist, of Partick; and Dr. Lyle, when he wrote the song already mentioned in 1780, also referred to it. When the lands of Gilmorehill were acquired an attempt was made to find its source, but it was not till 1889 that it was discovered, about fifty yards from the river, bubbling up out of the solid rock. An analysis of the water, made by Dr. Tatlock, was as follows:—

THE PEOPLE'S MINERAL SPA.

ANALYSIS OF THIS WATER BY R. R. TATLOCK, ESQ., F.R.S.E., F.I.C., F.C.S.

	Grains per Gallon.
Carbonate of Lime,	17·15
Carbonate of Magnesia,	4·69
Sulphate of Lime,	12·28
Sulphate of Magnesia,	28·60
Sulphate of Soda,	6·63
Chloride of Sodium,	5·53
Nitrate of Soda,	None
Silica,	·28
Alumina,	·23
Organic matter,	·03
Total solid matter,	75·32
Ammonia, free,	·006
Do., albuminoid,	·004
Do., Total,	·010
Hardness (degrees)	55·31°

The water is free from contamination of every kind.

Glasgow, 21st November, 1889.

The ground round the spring was then enclosed, and a suitable drinking fountain erected, which received a large amount of patronage from the public. Unfortunately, in consequence of the railway operations, the spring has now completely dried up, only at least temporarily, it is to be hoped.

The International Exhibition of 1888, which was held upon the Clayslaps and Gilmorehill portions of the park, was, as is well known, a marked success in every way. The area of the buildings was 525,000 square feet, the cost and equipment of the same being about £84,000. The area of the pleasure grounds was nearly 64 acres. The total number of visitors was 5,748,179, and the total drawings £225,928,—the clear surplus of income over expenditure being more than £40,000. A considerable sum was spent by the Exhibition authorities in deepening and purifying the Kelvin, which has had the practical result of permanently improving the river. The only trace of the Exhibition now remaining is the foundation work of the fairy fountain, which has been converted into an attractive flower garden. The site of the Bishop's Palace—a clever imitation of an old Glasgow city mansion of several centuries ago—is marked by a group of wych elm trees and a printed tablet west of the bandstand.

Near, also, to the fairy fountain is the bandstand, where are held the musical performances which are now such a valuable adjunct to the city parks. Concerts take place twice a-week during the summer months, the average attendance being about 6,000 persons.

The show of flowers in Kelvingrove Park is, as a rule, very good. At first the only flower garden was round the Stewart Fountain,—the site of the old garden of Kelvingrove House. Another area of ground was afterwards set apart for flowers on the opposite side of the carriage drive, where a series of geometrical flower plots was laid off. When the lake was formed these flower plots were transferred to their present site in front of Royal Terrace. During each year about 80,000 plants and bulbs are bedded out in the different flower gardens. A few years ago the idea was originated of giving away to the citizens all the surplus plants which were lifted from the flower beds at the end of the season. The experiment proved very successful, and is now carried out at all the parks, the demand being greater than the supply, thus shewing the growing interest taken in plants and flowers by all classes.

The casual passer-by in the park, as a general rule, takes but little notice of bird life, unless it is the song of the thrush which attracts his attention; but the following list of birds, which have been observed during recent years, may, perhaps, tend to increase the public interest in them,—an interest which has been awakened of late years by the water-fowl on the lake. The list has been compiled by Mr. J. MacNaught Campbell, the assistant curator at the Museum, and is a proof of the close attention with which he has studied the subject:—

1. Merlin, *Falco æsalon*, Gmelin.—Twice seen, once near the fountain in 1877, when in pursuit of a blackbird, and in 1880, feeding on a sparrow on Gilmorehill side.
2. Kestrel, *Falco tinnunculus*, L.—Frequently seen. In 1886 one frequented the park for several weeks, coursing up and down the Kelvin Valley.
3. Sparrow Hawk *Accipiter nisus*, L.—In the summer of 1887 one was noticed in pursuit of a pigeon, but, being frightened, flew off in the Hillhead direction.
4. Barn Owl, *Aluco flammeus*, L.—Occasionally seen. During 1887 and 1888 one (or a pair) was frequently seen in the evenings; but they have not been noticed since the Exhibition.
5. Dipper, *Cinclus aquaticus*, Bechstein.—Occasionally seen in the Kelvin. One was killed in the Park in 1891.
6. Mistletoe Thrush, *Turdus viscivorus*, L.—Not uncommon, and occasionally found breeding.
7. Song Thrush, *Turdus musicus*, L.—Breeds in the Park, but owing to the number of wandering cats the young are not often reared.
8. Redwing, *Turdus iliacus*, L.—A regular winter visitor.
9. Fieldfare, *Turdus pilaris*, L.—A regular winter visitor.
10. Blackbird, *Turdus merula*, L.—Breeds in the park.
11. Hedge Sparrow, *Accentor modularis*, L.—Breeds still in the park, but not so numerous as formerly.
12. Redbreast, *Erithacus rubecula*, L.—Common, and found breeding.
13. Redstart, *Ruticilla phœnicurus*, L.—Once seen on Gilmorehill.
14. Willow Wren, *Phylloscopus trochilus*, L.—Not seen since 1880.
15. Golden-crested Wren, *Regulus cristatus*, K. L. Koch.—Seen at Queen's Rooms Gate in the shrubbery, in 1876, and every year since.

16. Wren, *Troglodytes parvulus*, K. L. Koch.—Not common.
16A. Great Titmouse, *Parus major*, L.—Seen during winter.
17. Blue Titmouse, *Parus cæruleus*, L.—Common, and breeds in the park.
18. Long-tailed Titmouse, *Acredula caudata*, L.—Occasionally seen in the winter feeding on the meat put out behind the Museum for the birds.
19. Pied Wagtail, *Motacilla lugubris*, Temminck.—Common.
20. Grey Wagtail, *Motacilla sulphurea*, Bechstein.—Very common.
21. Yellow Wagtail, *Motacilla raii*, Bonaparte.—Common.
22. Tree Pipit, *Anthus trivialis*, L.—Occasionally seen.
23. Meadow Pipit, *Anthus pratensis*, L.—Not uncommon.
24. Skylark, *Alauda arvensis*, L.—Not now so common, but occasionally seen.
25. Snow Bunting, *Plectrophanes nivalis*, L.—A winter visitant, often in large flocks.
26. Reed Bunting, *Emberiza schæniclus*, L.—A pair bred and reared young not 150 yards from the bandstand in 1892.
27. The Bunting, *Emberiza miliaria*, L.—Not common, but sometimes seen.
28. Yellow Bunting, *Emberiza citrinella*, L.—Frequent.
29. Chaffinch, *Fringilla cœlebs*, L.—Common, and found breeding.
30. House Sparrow, *Passer domesticus*, L.—Too common. A piebald breed has been for years in the park.
31. Greenfinch, *Coccothraustes chloris*, L.—Very common.
32. Lesser Redpoll, *Linota rufescens*, Vieill.—Not often seen.
33. Linnet, *Linota cannabina*, L.—Not often seen, but a pair bred, in 1892, near the fountain.
34. Starling, *Sturnus vulgaris*, L.—Common.
35. Rook, *Corvus frugilegus*, L.—Common, bred up till 1889.
36. The Daw, *Corvus monedula*, L.—Common, breeds on chimneys and spires in the neighbourhood.
37. The Pie, *Pica rustica*, Scopoli.—Not seen since 1879.
38. Swallow, *Hirundo rustica*, L.—Common.
39. Swift, *Cypselus apus*, L.—Common.

40. The Nightjar, *Caprimulgus Europæus*, L.—Heard its note one night, in 1876, on Gilmorehill side.
41. Kingfisher, *Alcedo ispida*, L.—Has occasionally been seen, but not since 1887. A pair which bred on the island at Partick Bridge, in 1865, are in the Museum.
42. Common Partridge, *Perdix cinerea*, Latham.—Once only seen, probably a strayed one.
43. Land Rail or Corn Crake, *Crex pratensis*, Bechstein.—A nest found on Gilmorehill side in 1868. Not seen since.
44. Water Rail, *Rallus aquaticus*, L.—Twice seen in Kelvin since 1875.
45. Moor-Hen or Water-Hen, *Gallinula chloropus*, L.—Last one killed in park, in 1883, is now in Museum. Once seen since then.
46. Common Coot, *Fulica atra*, L.—Three times seen in Kelvin since 1875.
47. Lapwing or Peewit, *Vanellus vulgaris*, Bechstein.—Last seen in park in 1887.
48. Woodcock, *Scolopax rusticula*, L.—One was seen, in 1875, flying over the Prince of Wales Bridge.
49. Common Snipe, *Gallinago cœlestis*, Frenzel.—Sometimes seen. One killed against telegraph wire in park, in 1881, is now in Museum.
50. Common Sandpiper, *Totanus hypoleucus*, L.—Frequently seen. One in Museum, killed in 1884.
51. Common Redshank, *Totanus calidris*, L.—Occasionally seen on the Kelvin below the weir.
52. Common Curlew, *Numenius arquata*, L.—Sometimes seen flying overhead, but seldom alights.
53. The Common Tern, *Sterna fluviatilis*, Naumann.—One killed in park in 1892, now in Museum.
54. Black-headed Gull, *Larus ridibundus*, L.—Common all the year round.
55. Lesser Black-backed Gull, *Larus fuscus*, L.—Sometimes seen during stormy weather.
56. Kittiwake Gull, *Rissa tridactyla*, L.—Occasionally seen in Kelvin, especially in bad weather.

57. Common Guillemot, *Uria troile*, L.—One found newly dead in the park, in 1892, after a storm.
58. Little Grebe, *Podiceps fluviatilis*, Tunstall.—Seen occasionally in Kelvin; last one seen 1st February, 1892.
59. Common Heron, *Ardea cinerea*, L.—Frequently seen flying overhead, but does not often alight.
60. Canada Goose, *Bernicla Canadensis*, L.—Once seen on Kelvin in 1875, probably an escape.
61. Mute Swan, *Cygnus olor*, Gmelin.—Six individuals circled round the park one morning in 1884, and the species has twice been seen overhead since.
62. Mallard, or Wild Duck, *Anas boscas*, L.—Several times seen in Kelvin.
63. Teal, *Querquedula crecca*, L.—Sometimes seen in Kelvin. A male has frequented the pond for the last three years, and kept company with the tame water-fowl.
64. Red-breasted Merganser, *Mergus serrator*, L.—One seen in Kelvin, behind Museum, in 1877.

The artificial lake to the west of the Museum originated in the acquisition of some water-fowl by the Parks and Galleries Committee, which were supplemented by donations of swans and other birds from various private gentlemen. Their quarters in the Kelvin not being of the most congenial kind, a suggestion was made to form a lake of purer water, and the result was the formation of the present lake on the site of a similar feature in Sir Joseph Paxton's original design. In Sir Joseph's design the river is diverted to form the lake, and retains the same level throughout; but in the present lake the level is several feet higher than the river, and is supplied by the overflow from the Stewart Fountain. The islet in the centre is said to be a model in shape of the Island of Cyprus; which island, at the time of the formation of the lake, was very much before the public in a political way. This change in the features of the park has proved a very happy one, the birds being a source of never-ending attraction to the public, who have shown a commendable interest in their welfare and protection. So much has this been the case, that only one or two instances are on record of any wanton injury, except by rats and cats. While the great majority of our fancy native water-fowl are to be found, there are also several exotic species from the Far East and the Antipodes, including the Black Swan of Australia, the Mandarin Duck of China, the Whistling Teal of India, and other foreign breeds, which mingle with our better-known geese and ducks in friendly groups.

WATER-FOWL IN KELVINGROVE PARK.

*Moorhen, *Gallinula chloropus*, L.
Indian Gallinule, *Porphyrio neglectus*, Schlegel.—From India.
Black-headed Gull, *Larus ridibundus*, L.
Great Black-backed Gull, *Larus marinus*, L.
Lesser Black-backed Gull, *Larus fuscus*, L.
Herring Gull, *Larus argentatus*, Gmelin.
Kittiwake Gull, *Rissa tridactyla*, L.
Common Heron, *Ardea cinereus*, L.
White Stork, *Ciconia alba*, Bechstein.
*Wild or Grey Lag Goose, *Anser cinereus*, Meyer.
*Toulouse Goose, *Anser cinereus*, Meyer.—Variety.

Bernacle Goose, *Bernicla leucopsis*, Bechstein.
Brent Goose, *Bernicla brenta*, Pallas.
*Canada Goose, *Bernicla Canadensis*, L.
*Chinese Goose, *Anser cygnoides*, L., brown variety.—Native of China.
*Chinese Goose, *Anser cygnoides*, L., white variety.—Native of China.
*Common or Mute Swan, *Cygnus olor*, Gmelin.
Black Swan, *Cygnus atratus*, Latham.—Native of Australia.
Common Sheld Duck, *Tadorna cornuta*, S. G. Gmelin.
*Mallard or Wild Duck, *Anas boscas*, L.
*Common Duck, ⎫
*Aylesbury Duck, ⎬ Varieties of *Anas boscas*, L.
*Call Duck, ⎪
*Kayuga Duck, ⎭
Shoveller, *Spatula clypeata*, L.
Pintail Duck, *Dafila acuta*, L.
Chilian Pintail Duck, *Dafila spinicauda*, Vieill.
Teal, *Querquedula crecca*, L.
Wigeon, *Mareca penelope*, L.
Whistling Teal, *Dendrocygna javanica*, Horsf.—From India.
Mandarin Duck, *Aix galericulata*, L.—Native of China.
*Muscovy Duck, *Cairina moschata*, L.—Native of South America.

Those marked thus * have bred.
All are British species when not otherwise stated.

MAMMALS IN KELVINGROVE PARK.†

Common Bat, *Scotophilus pipistrellus*, Geoffroy.—Common.
Daubenton's Bat, *Vespertilio Daubentonii*, Leisler.—One was taken in 1879, and, as it has also been caught in Glasgow Green, it may be more common than is supposed.
Long-eared Bat, *Plecotus auritus*, L.—Occasionally seen.
Common Mole, *Talpa Europœa*, L.—One was found newly killed on Gilmorehill grounds in 1877, but not seen since.
Common Shrew, *Sorex vulgaris*, L.—Several times seen.

† For list of Fishes and Reptiles, see Appendix.

Water Shrew, *Sorex fodiens*, Pall.—What was taken to be an individual of this species was seen once, some years since, under the little wooden bridge which formerly stood near Museum.

Hedgehog, *Erinaceus Europæus*, L.—Several times found, but, as it is often kept as a pet, they may have been escapes.

Common Otter, *Lutra vulgaris*, Erxleb.—Has been twice seen in the Kelvin within the park since 1876.

Cat, *Felis catus*, L.—Feral animals of the domestic variety are only too common, and cause great destruction among the birds.

Common Fox, *Vulpes vulgaris*, Briss.—One was chased, some years ago, through the park and killed, it is understood, about Partick.

Common Squirrel, *Sciurus vulgaris*, L.—In 1885 one was seen among the trees in the Beech Walk for several days.

Long-tailed Field Mouse, *Mus sylvaticus*, L.—Has been several times seen.

Common Mouse, *Mus musculus*, L.—Common.

Brown Rat, *Mus decumanus*, Pall.—Too common. Great swarms were left after the Exhibition in 1888, and have been most destructive to the water-fowl. 11 young were taken in one nest behind the Museum in 1889!

Water Vole, *Arvicola amphibius*, Desmar.—Once or twice noticed. The common rat is often mistaken for this species.

Common Field Vole, *Arvicola agrestis*, L.—Has been seen once or twice only.

Common Hare, *Lepus timidus*, Linn.—An occasional visitor, but is not allowed to remain long, for obvious reasons.

Rabbit, *Lepus cuniculus*, L.—The same remark as above applies to this species.

DOMESTIC SPECIES.

Iceland Sheep, *Ovis aries*, L.—Variety. A ram of this breed is kept in the park. It was presented by Mr. James Young, Contractor.

Soa or Iceland Sheep, *Ovis aries*, L.—Variety. One or two of this breed were formerly in the park, but now only one, a ewe, which was born in 1888, within the Exhibition grounds.

The colony of crows, which were such a special attraction of the park for many years, deserve a short notice. In 1855, when the rookery was at its largest, there would be about 150 nests, principally in the large trees around Kelvingrove House and in the beech avenue leading from Kelvingrove Gate, with a few outsiders in trees in Kelvingrove Street and Sauchiehall Street. It appears that prior to 1842 a large rookery existed round the residence of Mr. James Ewing at the top of Queen Street. His property was acquired by the Edinburgh and Glasgow Railway, and in the course of their operations for making the present Queen Street Station the trees surrounding his house were cut down. The crows had no alternative but to move their quarters, which they, accordingly, did to Kelvingrove Park. The late Dr. Gillan of Inchinnan, who was at that time minister of St. John's Parish Church, made a humorous and sarcastic allusion to this fact in a speech which he delivered in the City Hall. The movement was just then beginning among the city churches for a change westward, and Dr. Gillan remarked, with that quaint humour which was so characteristic of him, that evidently it must be fashionable, because the very crows had taken up the idea and removed from Queen Street to Kelvingrove.

When the rookery was at its best, in 1856, a pair of

ravens from some of the neighbouring hills paid the crows a flying visit early one morning during the hatching season. The visit was not by any means a friendly one, for it meant a raid upon the eggs and the young birds, and the disastrous effects were quite evident next morning, from the number of dead unfledged birds which were found on the walks and under the trees. The crows were taken quite unawares, there being a great commotion among them, and it was some little time before the intruders were beaten off. After this a look-out was stationed on the tall poplar trees already referred to, which towered high above all the other trees in the grove. The ravens returned on two subsequent mornings, but the crows were always prepared for them, and eventually they were completely conquered, and had to retreat rather hastily, a company of the crows seeing them safely out of their territory.

Since 1856 the rookery has gradually, but steadily, declined—the last nest being seen in 1891. Various causes may be assigned for their disappearance, the chief, however, being the want of suitable healthy trees upon which they could build, for it is a well-known fact that a crow will not build its nest upon a rotten or unhealthy tree. There are numbers of them, however, which frequent the park daily, especially in severe weather, when they are fed along with the other birds. It is not easy to say to what particular place the crows have migrated, but probably a considerable number of them have found their way to the rookeries at Jordanhill, the Botanic Gardens, and Camphill.

For the last two years the appearance of the park has been much disfigured by the operations of the Caledonian Railway Company, in connection with their underground line from the East-End to the West-End of the city. These works, however, are now nearly completed, and it is to be hoped that many years will elapse before such a cutting-up of the park takes place again. Such operations are, doubtless, sometimes necessary, and, as a rule, the destruction which they entail can be redressed, but when they pass through a public park the damage which follows their track can never be properly effaced. It is to be regretted that the railway company did not so plan the line as to have had a station at one of the main entrances, as, if this could have been done, it would have been an immense boon to the citizens.

The new Museum and Art Galleries, which are in course of erection on the site of the Exhibition buildings, and the funds for which received their nucleus from the Exhibition surplus already referred to, will materially alter and improve the aspect of that portion of the park; but one section of the community will regret that this site has been fixed upon, as it has deprived the young and rising generation of almost the only available piece of recreation ground in the West-End of the city. The authorities, however, may see their way to secure a permanent place for the purpose; but if they intend to do so, they should not lose much time, as there are not many unbuilt lots of ground left in the vicinity.

KELVINGROVE HOUSE.

III.

QUEEN'S PARK AND CAMPHILL.

THE Queen's Park, which was formerly known as Pathhead Farm, was acquired by the City of Glasgow from the late Mr. Neale Thomson of Camphill, in the year 1857. The price paid was £30,000, and the area of the estate at that time was about 143 acres. Mr. Thomson had purchased the farm, a few years previously, from Sir John Maxwell of Pollok, and he handed it over to the Corporation for the sum he had paid for it, without taking any profit on the transaction. In thus aiding the city to acquire such a valuable property, so well suited for the purpose for which it was intended, Mr. Thomson undoubtedly conferred a great boon on Glasgow. The proposal at the time found many opponents in the Council, who looked upon the site as too far distant from the city; but time has shown that the promoters of the scheme (who received considerable aid from several forcible articles in the *Glasgow Herald* by the then editor, the late Mr. James Pagan) were wise in offering inducements towards the opening up of the outskirts of the city. The tenant of Pathhead Farm, when it was bought by the Corporation, was Mr. William Finlay, who occupied it for upwards of half-a-century, and who was well known as one of the most successful farmers in the neighbourhood of Glasgow.

Immediately after the Corporation had got possession of the lands they called in Sir John Paxton to advise them as to laying it out, and requested him to furnish a plan and report, and to submit an estimate of the probable cost. The report which Sir Joseph gave was most favourable, and his views and plans were carried out as far as the laying-out of the grounds was concerned. There was one point, however, upon which Sir Joseph gave a very strong opinion—viz., the erection of a Winter Garden there; and it may not be out of place to insert here the views of that eminent landscape gardener on the subject. Sir Joseph, in his report, said,—

"Having had many parks to lay out, and having visited "nearly all the public parks in Europe, it has always "occurred to me that there was a want of what I consider "ought to be an essential feature in such places of resort— "viz., a covered building to shelter visitors from the "weather, and which should also be an attractive object "in itself. In our climate especially it often happens that "those who go out for recreation and exercise are over-

"taken by rain, and having no place of shelter, suffer
"serious inconvenience, and, frequently, instead of de-
"riving the benefit to their health of which they went in
"search, are laid up, for several days, from the effects of
"cold and wet, and sometimes sustain permanent injury to
"their health. I have, accordingly, provided in my design
"for the erection of a handsome, but not expensive build-
"ing, which will entirely obviate this difficulty. I propose
"the central part of the building to be used for a variety
"of purposes. Its general use I would recommend to be
"as a museum for works of art, and it could also be
"appropriated to periodical exhibitions, musical promen-
"ades, and various other purposes during the summer.
"I propose to cover the two wings with glass, and to plant
"a good-sized border at the back of each with plants from
"Australia, China, the Himalayas, and other temperate
"climes, so as to form a beautiful screen to the back wall,
"and at the same time leave room for a promenade of
"sufficient width to make a most agreeable resort at all
"seasons. The plants would be such as to require very
"little expense or care to keep in order. The end
"buildings would be appropriated for refreshment-rooms
"and cloak-rooms, and provided with other necessary
"conveniences, and a rental would be derived from letting
"them to a contractor."

The landscape design of this building can be seen in the office of the City Engineer, City Chambers.

The sum which Sir Joseph Paxton estimated would be required for laying out the park according to the plans submitted by him, was £29,847, which included the cost of the buildings mentioned in his report, and which he put down at £12,000. After the subject had been carefully considered in the Council, the Master of Works (the late Mr. John Carrick) was instructed to prepare plans of the whole property, shewing a scheme for feuing the margin of the park. This scheme was ultimately adopted, and involved an actual outlay of £28,350 in laying-out the grounds, in addition to a considerable sum spent during the two previous years in levelling, draining, and other similar operations preparatory to the actual formation of the park. The erection of the Winter Garden and the construction of a proposed artificial lake were postponed, and both of these schemes have, since that time, remained in abeyance. The plan submitted by Mr. Carrick has been almost entirely carried out, and included the continuation of Eglinton Street right through the Corporation lands of Coplawhill, and the properties belonging to Hutchesons' Hospital, and that of Mr. Dixon, thus opening up their ground for feuing purposes between Cathcart Road and Pollokshaws Road. The old Langside

Queens Park, looking west.

Road, which formerly went right over the Pathhead Hill, past the farm-house, was altered to curve round the base of it, and forms the boundary-line of the park proper from the recreation ground.

The actual laying-out of the park was commenced in the year 1857, and a considerable part of the work, in its initial stages, was carried out by the unemployed during the years 1858 and 1859. The site proposed by Sir Joseph Paxton for the Winter Garden was on the terrace, and is now utilized as a flower garden. The formation of this handsome esplanade, which is 750 feet long by 140 feet wide, with terraces and a commanding granite stair, has entirely changed and improved the appearance of this part of the park from a landscape point of view. The park was formally opened to the public on 11th September, 1862, by the late Bailie Gemmell, the Convener of the Park Committee, who, in commemoration of the event, planted a chestnut tree at what is now the entrance to the Wellcroft Bowling Green, and it is still fresh and flourishing.

The old farm-house of Pathhead, which was situated on the eastern rise of the hill, has been retained, and now forms convenient waiting-rooms for the public. Adjoining are the plant and tool houses, along with a commodious house for the head gardener. An artificial mound, with a handsome flag-pole, has been raised on the summit immediately opposite the old Caledonian Camp, on the lands of Camphill. The elevation here above the sea level is 209 feet. The view from this point is unsurpassed in the immediate neighbourhood of Glasgow, and from no other situation can the great City and Strathclyde be seen to greater advantage. In the foreground lie Pollokshaws; Cathcart, with its church and old castle; Rutherglen and Castlemilk, where tradition says that Queen Mary rested before her defeat at Langside in 1568. The view of the distant landscape is equally interesting, and includes the Kilpatrick hills and Campsie range, the Vale of Clyde as far as Lanark, Cathkin Braes, Neilston Pad, Gleniffer Braes, Ballygeich, the Mearns moors, Lochgoin, &c.

Considerable historical interest attaches to the park, and especially to the adjoining estate of Camphill. This property was acquired by the grandfather of the late Mr. Neale Thomson, and remained in the possession of the family till 1866, when it was sold to the patrons of Hutcheson's Hospital for £24,428. About the beginning of this century the present large and commodious house was built, and the gardens and grounds laid out. The estate takes its name from the old circular camp on the top of the hill. Rather a curious and important discovery was made there some time ago, as noticed in the *Glasgow Herald* of July 15, 1867, from which the following is a quotation:—

"The hill formed an important military position in "connection with the battle of Langside. Its name, "however, is due to much earlier associations, being "evidently derived from the existence on its summit of "what appear to be the remains of an ancient fort or "encampment. These remains consist of huge grass-"grown mounds, which are supposed to have at one "time formed part of a defensive work, encircling the "brow of the hill. Along the north-east side the ridge "is nearly continuous, but towards the south only a few "detached hillocks remain, with wide gaps between,— "the position of these, however, being quite consistent "with the supposition that they are fragments of a circular "rampart. The enclosed area measures some 300 feet "in diameter. It slopes to the south-west; and its "surface, which is irregular, is covered with beech trees "of many years' growth. By general consent the place "is allowed to have been the site of an ancient camp. "In old books of topography we find it spoken of as "a Roman camp; but some antiquaries, we understand, "are rather inclined to the opinion that the remains are "of Caledonian origin. Be this as it may, we refer to "the subject at present for the purpose of noticing a

"curious discovery which was recently made on the
"ground. It may readily be supposed that the old hill-
"top, with its traditions, has always been an interesting
"subject of speculation for the inhabitants of Camphill
"House. A few months ago, we understand, certain
"members of Mrs. Thomson's family bethought them
"of having an excavation made, with the view of ascer-
"taining whether any relics of the olden time existed
"below the surface. Mr. Hamilton, the overseer on the
"estate, who has himself always taken a lively interest
"in the camp, was taken into counsel, and under his
"superintendence the proposed operation was carried
"out. A trench was cut into the slope, not far from
"the centre of the enclosure, the spademen being in-
"structed to work downwards till they reached the hard
"subsoil, which had evidently never been disturbed
"before. This point was reached at a depth of about
"four feet, and the trench was then pushed forward in
"a longitudinal direction. By-and-by the men came to
"a place where the hard bottom seemed to dip away,
"and following the indication thus given they worked
"down to a lower level. After getting to a depth of
"about eight feet from the surface, they began to turn
"up pieces of charred wood, together with quantities of
"a substance which Mr. Hamilton, on examination,

"identified as half-burned grain. On making this dis-
"covery the excavation was cautiously proceeded with,
"and the result was, that after the removal of the *debris*
"there was laid bare a sort of floor, paved with rough
"stones, measuring about twelve feet long by six feet
"in breadth. The paved surface resembled a wide
"shallow trough, sinking in the middle and rising at the
"two sides, and having an upward slope towards the
"north end to the extent of about a foot in the entire
"length. Over this surface there lay what may best
"be described as a cake of charred oaten grains, mixed
"with pieces of oak in a similar condition. A portion
"of the corn had been reduced to the state of dark
"brown powder; but many of the grains, though charred
"to blackness, still preserved their shape, while, on some,
"even the remains of the husk could be plainly dis-
"tinguished. The spot in which the discovery was made
"was minutely examined, but no traces of building were
"found, nor, indeed, anything recognisable as man's
"handiwork, with the exception of the rudely-paved floor
"just described. The pieces of wood turned up were
"all more or less burned on the surface, but internally
"presented a sound and undecayed appearance, though
"almost as black in colour as the well-known Irish bog-
"oak. Mr. Hamilton has preserved specimens both of

"the wood and of the grain. He has also in his pos-
"session a primitive-looking old mill-stone or quern,
"which was found, many years ago, near the margin of
"the camp. With regard to the interesting discovery to
"which we have called attention it is not for us to
"speculate. The most natural supposition would seem
"to be that the rude stone floor formed part of an
"ancient kiln used for the drying of grain. But what
"may have been the construction of such kiln, and
"whether it belonged to the Caledonians or their Roman
"invaders, we must leave it for antiquaries to determine."

Specimens of the grain and wood may be seen at the Kelvingrove Museum. Mr. Cairns of the Queen's Park Collegiate School has also some of the charred grain, and the quaint old mill-stone or quern, with many other relics of old Glasgow.

The battle of Langside is supposed to have taken place on the slopes of the park, and particularly in the lane now appropriately called Battlefield Road. Here a memorial monument was erected by public subscription, chiefly through the exertions of the late Mr. Alex. M. Scott, the recent historian of the battle and neighbourhood. When the farm of Pathhead was made a public park the name of Queen's Park was given to it, to commemorate that notable event in Scottish history.

Queen's Park, Keeper's house.

Queen's Park, Carpet Bed.

The public have, for many years, been desirous that the ancient camp at Camphill should become the property of the City and be added to the park. Various meetings, from time to time, beginning in 1870, were held between the Parks Committee and the patrons of Hutchesons' Hospital, and numerous joint plans were prepared by the engineers of the respective Trusts, showing less or more ground for park or feuing purposes, and how excambions could be made in part payment. It is only recently, however, that this beautiful property has been acquired by the City, chiefly owing to the impetus given to the renewed negotiations for its purchase by the extension of the southern boundary of Glasgow to the River Cart by the Act of 1891, and thereby including the ground. On the 24th March, 1893, the patrons of Hutchesons' Hospital offered to sell to the Town Council the whole of the Camphill property at the price of £63,000, and on the 4th May thereafter the Parks and Galleries Trustees of the Corporation, on the motion of Councillor Sinclair, seconded by Bailie Bilsland, agreed to accept the offer. In the case of both sellers and buyers the motions were carried by large majorities, while in the case of the Hospital patrons there were, of the *non*-Town Councillors, for the offer to sell more than two to one. The price asked was made up by 4 per cent. compound interest on the £24,428, the sum paid by the Hutcheson Trust in 1866, added to that capital. The extent of the ground is 58 acres, less 1½ poles.

The atmosphere at the Queen's Park is purer and freer from smoke and chemicals than any other part of the city, and, the prevalent winds being from the south and southwest, is likely to remain so. Meteorological observations show that this district has less rainfall than any part of Renfrewshire, in which it was formerly included, although now it is a part of the County of Glasgow City, the average rainfall for the last fourteen years, as taken at the Queen's Park, 144 feet above sea level, being 32·29 inches, and average temperature 45 degrees.

As already stated, the near and distant views from Queen's Park are very fine, and unrivalled in or near Glasgow, and those from Camphill, on the north-west, west, and south-west, are not less beautiful, grand, and far-reaching. A few notes upon the natural beauties of this recently acquired property may be of interest to the citizens. It is specially rich in large ornamental timber trees, consisting of beech, birch, plane, elm, ash, and chestnut, and in evergreens, such as large masses of choice rhododendrons, and of hollies, both common and variegated. Dotted over the flower garden are handsome specimens of Irish and common yews, and of the *Cedrus deodora* and

Lebanii, or cedar of Lebanon. There is also a weeping ash, growing near the flower garden, 40 feet high, grafted by the late gardener, Mr. David Hamilton, one of the best specimens in the West of Scotland. There are growing in the conservatory a handsome specimen of the *Wisteria sinensis*, and also fine plants of the white and pink lapageria.

The flower garden is very unique, in the old Dutch style of 100 years ago, with straight grass and gravel walks. There are also two elegant arbours and several rustic vases. The collection of spring and old fashioned flowers in the old garden is very large and highly interesting. It may be mentioned that a rookery of crows has made a commencement in the trees at Camphill, near the garden. In 1887 there were only five nests, whereas this year they numbered over fifty. Now that they have left their old quarters in Kelvingrove Park, they should be encouraged, as much as possible, to remain at Camphill. The song birds are also very numerous, the cuckoo being a yearly visitor, this being the only locality so near the city that this welcome harbinger of spring visits.

With regard to the laying out of the new portion of the park, there are some four or five acres, including the flower garden, plant houses, part of the kitchen garden, and large bowling green, which are admirably suited for being set apart as a place of instruction and amusement in the shape of an arboretum, gymnasium, and also a maze, such as exists at Hampton Court and Hatfield. The old garden should certainly be preserved, as there are few specimens near Glasgow which show so well what the old-fashioned gardens of our country houses used to be. A considerable portion of the lower ground is well suited for feuing purposes, for which a large sum could be obtained, and which would not detract in any way from the natural beauties and amenities of the Park. It would be desirable to continue the present carriage drive in the Queen's Park round the north and west side of the camp, and connect it with the Camphill drive round the base of the hill to Langside.

The prevailing winds here blow nine months of the year from west by north and west, consequently vegetation, to a considerable extent, escapes the noxious smoke from the large manufacturing works all over the city. This fact accounts for the healthiness of trees, shrubs, and flowers, as compared with the other parks. Some 70,000 plants and bulbs are bedded out here every season. A band performs twice a-week from May till September, the average attendance being 5,000 persons. A census of visitors to the park was taken on the 26th August, 1892, when the large number of 43,300 entered by the several gates. A large portion of the park is set apart for recreation,—

one large field of 22 acres for football and cricket, and several smaller enclosures for children. There are upon the property two large bowling greens and lawn tennis courts, let to clubs at moderate rents.

With the large addition of Camphill grounds to this park, it is to be hoped that the Parks Committee may see their way soon to carry out Sir Joseph Paxton's scheme of winter garden and ornamental lake, either according to the original plan and site, or in some other part of this large ornamental and useful public park. The mansion-house of Camphill could be utilized as a museum, or for some other public purpose.

CAMPHILL HOUSE.

IV.

ALEXANDRA PARK.

ALEXANDRA PARK was purchased in 1866 by the City Improvement Trustees from Mr. Walter Stewart of Haghill, under special powers conferred upon them by their Act. The object for which it was acquired was to provide a park and recreation ground for the north-eastern section of the city, and after it was laid out by the Trustees it was handed over to the city, thus becoming one of the public parks. In common with the other city parks, it is now maintained out of the assessments levied under the Parks and Galleries Act.

The property extended from the Monkland Canal to the Cumbernauld Road, and was known as Wester Kennyhill, which had been in the possession of the Stewart family for several generations, principally for agricultural purposes. There was, however, an extensive distillery at the north-east corner of the property where the golf-house at present stands. At the time when it was purchased it was a cold, bare, and bleak hill, with very few trees upon it.

Alexandra Park

From some of the higher points there is a commanding and extensive view. On a clear day Ben Lomond can be seen, as well as the hills round Loch Katrine, the Campsie range, and the Kilpatrick hills, whilst to the south there is a good view of the Cathkin Braes and the Vale of Clyde, with Tinto in the distance. The position at first appeared rather isolated, being nearly a mile from the dwelling-houses on the outskirts of the city; but, as in the case of the Queen's Park, whenever the ground was laid out and the park was formed, building operations commenced in its vicinity, and a new outlet was found for the ever-increasing population.

Mr. Alexander Dennistoun, the proprietor of the adjoining estate of Golfhill, acted in a very liberal manner towards the City Improvement Trustees. He gifted to the park five acres of land near the south-west corner, thus bringing it in touch with the Alexandra Parade, which now forms its principal entrance. This parade, which makes a magnificent approach, is not only of great public benefit, in affording an easy access for the citizens to their park, but has also proved of the greatest use to Mr. Dennistoun himself, in opening up his own property for feuing purposes,—a property which has been laid out in the most generous spirit as regards wide streets and open spaces, and is now known as the suburb of Dennistoun.

The total area of the park was then eighty-five acres, including Mr. Dennistoun's gift, already referred to. After the purchase had been completed, no time was lost in laying out the ground. Plans were prepared showing how the property could be utilized for both pleasure and profit—three sides of the Park being available for feuing purposes. It is to be noticed that in this respect the Corporation have shown great tact and carefulness in all their purchases of land for the use of the public, for in several cases the original purchase-money expended for parks has, in great part, been recouped by the able and skilful manner in which the feuing-ground round the various parks has been handled,—a result for which we are indebted principally to the watchful and wise guidance of the late Mr. John Carrick, City Architect and Master of Works.

During the years 1867 and 1868, which were noted for great depression in trade, several hundreds of unemployed starving artizans and labourers were employed in the initial work connected with the formation of the park, and the greater part of the actual laying-out was performed by them. Advantage was taken of an old disused freestone quarry near the canal, which was converted into an open swimming pond, 150 feet long by 80 feet broad, and of an oval shape. It is supplied with Loch Katrine water, and is surrounded by a dense plantation of willows and poplars. As the charge for admission is only a penny, it is largely taken advantage of during the summer months. In 1878, during five months, 59,947 persons paid for admission; and the average attendance per annum, since it was opened in 1877, has been 19,600.

The ancient and royal game of golf, which used to be played on Glasgow Green and at Golfhill, is a favourite pastime in the park; and whilst the course is not very long, nor the hazards difficult, a great amount of recreation is afforded to many of the citizens. Of late years the game has become exceedingly popular, and the only fear is, that as the numbers desiring to play are so numerous, and the space at the disposal of the golfers is so limited, some restrictions will require to be placed upon the players.

Near to the flower garden there is a miniature lake, with several islands in it, which have been well stocked with many kinds of fancy water-fowl. Both in this park and at Kelvingrove the water and the birds are unfailing sources of attraction to all visitors, especially to the children, who never seem to tire of watching and feeding the fowls. The following is a list of those at present upon the lake :—

*Moor-hen or Water-hen, *Gallinula chloropus*, L.
*Wild or Grey Lag Goose, *Anser cinereus*, Meyer.
*Common Goose, *Anser cinereus*, Meyer, variety.

Bernacle Goose, *Bernicla leucopsis*, Bechstein.
*Chinese Goose (white variety), *Anser cygnoides*, L.—Native of China.
 Common or Mute Swan, *Cygnus olor*, Gmelin.
*Black Swan, *Cygnus atratus*, Latham.—Native of Australia.
 Common Sheld Duck, *Tadorna cornuta*, S. G. Gmelin.
*Mallard or Wild Duck, *Anas boscas*, L.
*Common Duck, } Varieties of *Anas boscas*, L.
*Rouen Duck, }
 Teal, *Querquedula crecca*, L.
 Wigeon, *Mareca penelope*, L.
*Muscovy Duck, *Cairina moschata*, L.—Native of South America

Those marked (*) have bred.

Adjoining the lake an artificial pond has been formed for the sailing of model yachts, which is largely patronized by the rising generation, and forms a source of both pleasure and instruction. In this connection it may be mentioned that there is a model yacht club, which has its headquarters at the park. The club is in a flourishing condition, and during the summer months holds regattas, which are very successful. Accommodation is provided for the club, which enables the members to leave their yachts at the park, for which a small charge is made. Between the lake and the pond an ornamental bandstand has been erected, where musical performances take place once a-week during the summer months, the average attendance being about 1,800.

Considerable difficulty was experienced in planting the Park with trees and shrubs, which would be able to withstand the many gaseous and chemical fumes which impregnate the atmosphere in the eastern part of the city, and especially those which came from the Blochairn Ironworks, immediately to the west on the opposite side of the canal; but the efforts in this direction have been even more successful than one could have anticipated. As a rule, evergreen shrubs do not seem able to withstand the winter and smoke, with the exception of broad-leaved hollies, rhododendrons, and acubas. But many of the deciduous trees have done very well, and it is quite surprising to find how fresh and green the foliage continues during the greater part of the summer. Flowers also have succeeded remarkably well, and attain a considerable degree of perfection. About 60,000 plants and bulbs are annually bedded out, and in a good season there is quite a brilliant display of colour during the summer and autumn months. Every year additional facilities, both by rail and road, are being provided for getting access to the park, and, on 13th August, 1893, 15,810 persons entered by the several gates. As this is a park which is practically unknown to many inhabitants of the West-End, it may be mentioned that very frequent trains are run on the circular railway, which land the passengers at the Alexandra Park Station, within one minute's walk of the park gate.

The Parks Committee have recently acquired the lands of Easter Kennyhill, which are also part of the original

Cathkin Braes Park contains forty-nine acres. It is bounded on the south and east by the public road leading from Carmunnock to Rutherglen, Cambuslang, and East Kilbride, and on the west and north-west by the lands of Castlemilk. Cathkin House is situated a short distance to the east of the park, and was built in 1779. The estate originally extended along the sky range of the Cathkin Hills for several miles. The present proprietor, Mr. A. Crum Maclae, is the representative of three old and well-known Glasgow families—the Crums, Ewings, and Maclaes, who have all been more or less connected with the city and its prosperity. Castlemilk, a historical old house, with beautiful grounds, lies immediately to the west of the park. Part of the house is very old, and tradition says that the unfortunate Queen Mary slept there the night before the battle of Langside. The room which she occupied is still known as Queen Mary's room.

The park lies on a pleasantly undulating slope, with a northern exposure, about 600 feet above the sea level. It is richly clothed with natural wood, and there is an abundance of broom and other native undergrowth. According to the conditions of Mr. Dick's gift, the public are permitted to roam at will all over the grounds, seats being provided here and there, and swings for the amusement of the younger generation. Mr. Dick has also stipulated that

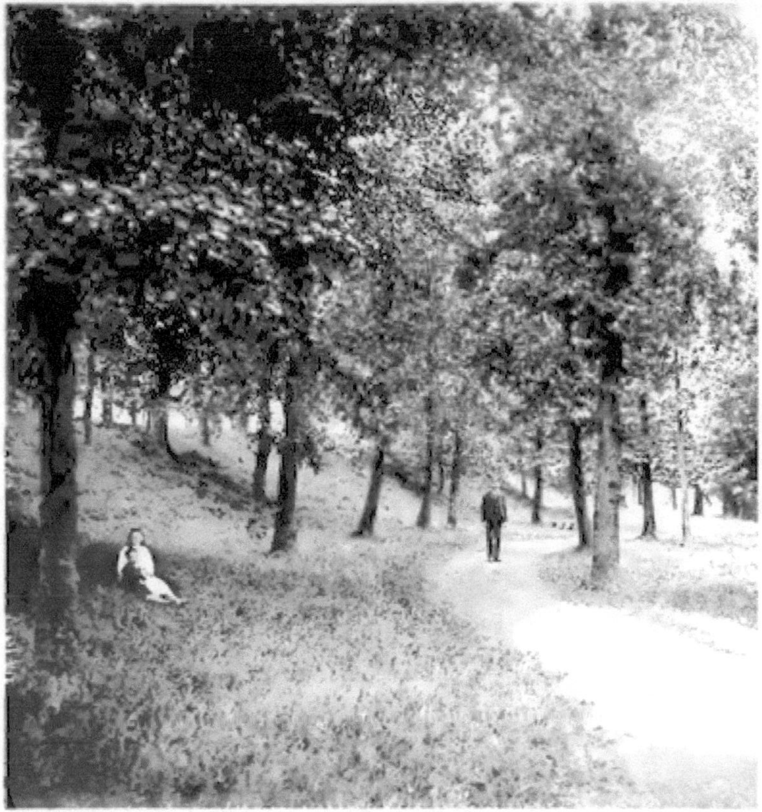

Cathkin Braes Park

On the lands of Castlemilk, where there is an attractive golf course rented by a club, there are the outlines of an ancient circular British camp still visible, after the lapse of many centuries.

Since the park was opened, eight years ago, the average number of visitors during the year has been about 150,000, principally during holidays and the summer months. It is interesting to note that the park is used largely for pic-nics connected with churches and schools,—a purpose for which it is admirably adapted. In this connection it may be pointed out that there is no place of shelter in the park for visitors,—a defect which certainly ought to be remedied. Musical performances are given during the Fair holidays, and the result has been a marked success. The real music of the park, however, is provided by the birds, of which the following is a list:—

   Merlin, *Falco æsalon*, Gm.
   Kestrel, *Falco tinnunculus*, L.
   Sparrow Hawk, *Accipiter nisus*, L.
   Tawny Owl, *Strix aluco*, L.
   Barn Owl, *Aluco flammeus*, L.
   Spotted Flycatcher, *Muscicapa grisola*, L.
   Mistletoe Thrush, *Turdus viscivorus*, L.
   Song Thrush, *Turdus musicus*, L.
   Redwing, *Turdus iliacus*, L.
   Fieldfare, *Turdus pilaris*, L.
   Blackbird, *Turdus merula*, L.
   Hedge Sparrow, *Accentor modularis*, L.

Redbreast, *Erithacus rubecula*, L.
Greater Whitethroat, *Sylvia rufa*, Bodd.
Blackcap, *Sylvia atricapilla*, L.
Wren, *Troglodytes parvulus*, K. L. Koch.
Great Titmouse, *Parus major*, L.
Blue Titmouse, *Parus cæruleus*, L.
Pied Wagtail, *Motacilla lugubris*, Temm.
Grey Wagtail, *Motacilla sulphurea*, Bech.
Yellow Wagtail, *Motacilla raii*, Bonap.
Skylark, *Alauda arvensis*, L.
Reed-Bunting, *Emberiza schœniclus*, L.
Common Bunting, *Emberiza miliaria*, L.
Yellow Hammer, *Emberiza citrinella*, L.
Chaffinch, *Fringilla cœlebs*, L.
House Sparrow, *Passer domesticus*, L.
Greenfinch, *Coccothraustes chloris*, L.
Goldfinch, *Carduelis elegans*, Stephens.
Lesser Redpoll, *Linota rufescens*, Vieill.
Linnet, *Linota cannobina*, Linn.
Bullfinch, *Pyrrhula Europœa*, Vieill.
Starling, *Sturnus vulgaris*, L.
Rook, *Corvus frugilegus*, L.
Jackdaw, *Corvus monedula*, L.
The Pie, *Pica rustica*, Scop.
Swallow, *Hirundo rustica*, L.
Cuckow, *Cuculus canorus*, L.
Wood Pigeon, *Columba palumbus*, L.
Pheasant, *Phasianus colchicus*, L.
Common Partridge, *Perdix cinerea*, Lath.
Land Rail, *Crex pratensis*, Bech.
Golden Plover, *Charadrius pluvialis*, L.
Lapwing, *Vanellus vulgaris*, Bech.

With regard to the means of access to the park, it may be mentioned that it is distant from the Royal Exchange, as the crow flies, about five miles. From Rutherglen, the distance by road is about two miles, and from Cathcart about two and a-half miles. To both of these places trains run every hour, and the walk to the park is charming. There is also a service of omnibuses from Rutherglen to Burnside, which pass within a short distance of the park. A continuation of the railway from Cathcart to Cambuslang has been for some time in contemplation, which, it is to be hoped, will be carried out. The park would then be brought in touch with all parts of the city.

VI.

THE BOTANIC GARDENS.

THE acquisition of the Botanic Gardens—now the property of the city, and therefore one of the public parks—is the most important step which the city has made, in recent years, in the way of acquiring open spaces for the benefit of the public. It is, in one sense, an experiment, but, at the same time, it will certainly prove that the Glasgow public have been trained to respect flowers and plants; and it should still further stimulate the authorities to cultivate, in their higher forms, the beneficial influences of horticulture.

The Glasgow Botanic Gardens have had a somewhat varied career. They originally existed in connection with the old University in the High Street, in a collection of plants almost exclusively having relation to medicine. However, the Gardens were ultimately removed to the West-End in 1817, and this may be regarded as the beginning of the present Institution. Ground was acquired between Claremont Street, Dumbarton Road, and Sauchiehall Street,—the practical founder being Mr. Thomas Hopekirk of Dalbeth, a gentleman who was passionately fond of botany, and who possessed a private collection of 3,000 plants, which he gifted to the Gardens. Under the patronage of the University, and chiefly owing to the influence of Mr. Hopekirk, Mr. R. Austin, and several other public-spirited citizens, a company was formed, and incorporated as the Royal Botanic Institution of Glasgow. About eight acres were purchased on the site above mentioned. The grounds were well suited for the purpose intended, and were laid out by the late Mr. Stewart Murray, who occupied the position of curator for many years. The Gardens were very successful from every point of view, and attained considerable reputation under the skilful guidance of Professor (afterwards Sir William) Hooker, the eminent botanist. In 1821, there were no fewer than 9,000 species in the Gardens.

For many years the Gardens formed the principal attraction to botanists and lovers of Nature in and around the city, but as building operations extended westward the locality became so congested, especially with public works towards the south, that the directors resolved, in 1838, to save their valuable collection of plants by moving the Gardens farther westward. Accordingly, in 1839, they purchased the present site from the trustees of the Kelvin-

Botanic Garden

side estate,—in all about twenty-five acres. The removal was commenced in 1839, and was completed in 1842. On the back wall of the eastmost house in Fitzroy Place there is a tablet with the following inscription upon it:—
"Glasgow Botanic Garden, Instituted 1817."

Up to this time (1842), and till the year 1891, the Gardens were a private undertaking, supported by subscriptions and entrance money, with this exception, however, that for several days in the summer free admission was granted to the working-classes, in terms of a gift to the Institution by the late Mr. William Campbell of Tullichewan.

The removal of the Gardens, in 1839, to their present site, and the consequent operations in connection therewith in the way of draining, fencing, erecting of plant-houses, &c., entailed considerable expenditure on the part of the directors. The debt thus incurred increased so much that in 1863 an appeal was made to the citizens, and about £8,000 was raised. This, however, was only sufficient to keep the Institution going for a short time; and in 1878 fresh difficulties presented themselves, as it became absolutely necessary to renew the plant-houses, which, having been removed from the old Gardens, were becoming dilapidated. Fortunately, assistance was once more at hand, as a handsome gift was made to the Institution by

Mr. William Ewing, which was available for building a most useful range of propagating plant-houses.

About this time an arrangement was made with the late Mr. John Kibble of Coulport, to remove and re-erect in the Gardens his large conservatory. Difficulties occurred in the working-out of the arrangement, and to avoid litigation the Institution appealed to the Town Council of Glasgow for assistance, who advanced a sufficient sum to enable the arrangement to be worked out, and also provided funds for the erection of the present handsome range of teak plant-houses.

Further financial difficulties still continued to hamper in every way the utility of the Gardens, and their indebtedness to the city of Glasgow increased so much that, in 1887, the city promoted a bill for the acquisition of the Gardens as a public park, and entered into actual possession in that year.

Thereafter certain technical difficulties intervened, which prevented the Gardens being actually thrown open as a public park; but with the passing of the Boundaries Extension Bill these difficulties were cleared away, and towards the end of 1891 the Gardens were opened free to the public, and ceased to be a private venture.

Now that the Gardens have become the property of the citizens, and that, too, at a very low figure, one should not forget the public-spirited citizens who spent, in a most generous way, their money towards accomplishing a most laudable object. The present ratepayer of Glasgow is paying nothing for the Botanic Gardens, so far as the original cost is concerned, as any advances which were made have all gone towards improvement and upkeep, and the city to-day is in possession of a valuable educational institution, which, at the same time, is an ornamental public park.

Since the Gardens came into the possession of the Corporation several improvements have suggested themselves in the way of making them available for larger masses of people than in the past. The ground on the north side of the Kelvin has been taken in, and it is intended to connect both sides by means of a light rustic bridge. The steep sloping banks on the north side of the river are well adapted for effective planting, and, as the Gardens are situated in a district of the city comparatively free from smoke, any improvements in this way should be successful.

At present the south banks are well clothed with natural wood; but, owing to the crippled finances of the Gardens for many years past, the directors wisely confined themselves to preserving, as far as possible, their wealth of hot-house plants, and had not the means of paying much attention to out-door matters beyond the upkeep of the valuable collection of medicinal plants and of the natural orders, which at present are very complete. It is to be hoped, however, that the Corporation will now place the Gardens on a thoroughly sound footing, and make them, as they ought to be, worthy of this great city.

The general collection of hot-house plants in the Gardens is very fine, embracing all the different sections and containing many splendid specimen plants. The tree ferns in the Winter Garden are worthy of special notice. Of economic plants, useful in arts and manufactures, there is a large and varied representation, which is of great interest in a manufacturing centre such as Glasgow. The collection of herbaceous plants is also very valuable, and was admirably laid out by the late curator, Mr. Robert Bullen, shortly after his appointment. It is especially interesting to those who study botany, and from it, as well as from the other collections in the Gardens, the necessary specimens for the use of the Professor of Botany in the University are supplied. Students are also offered every facility for practical observation and taking notes.

Reference has already been made to the large conservatory in the Gardens, which was formerly the property of Mr. Kibble. It was originally erected by him at his coast residence at Coulport, Loch Long, and, in 1871, was offered by him to the Gardens, subject to a lease of twenty-one years in his favour. This offer was accepted, and the conservatory was removed from Coulport and re-erected in the Gardens, with considerable additions and improvements. For some time it was chiefly used for concerts and public meetings, and the Earl of Beaconsfield and Mr. Gladstone both delivered their rectorial addresses to the students of Glasgow University in the building. Ultimately the lease was purchased by the Gardens, and the conservatory, or palace as it was then called, was transformed into a Winter Garden. The change was a happy one, and was admirably worked out. Many of the plants in the range of hot-houses had grown too large, and were transferred to this large building, where they could be seen to better advantage. The plan of laying-out has been most successful, and the result is a conservatory or covered promenade, which is second to none in the kingdom. As the public have now free admission, it will, doubtless, be largely taken advantage of, and will prove beyond doubt the great benefit of having similar buildings erected in each of our public parks. Both in Glasgow Green and the Queen's Park admirable sites are to be found, and, when once such buildings are erected and stocked with plants, the actual cost of upkeep is comparatively small, as there is little or no necessity for renewal of plants.

The extension of the Caledonian Railway Company, now in course of construction for the purpose of uniting the east and the west of the city, has, to a certain extent, cut up and defaced the Gardens. Fortunately, however, its track is visible only on the lower portion of the grounds, where few visitors walk; and after artistic lodges have been erected at the principal entrance from Great Western Road, and the curator has planted a screen of fast-growing trees to shut out the station and the railway cutting, the amenity of the Gardens will not be injured to any material extent. It should, at the same time, be remembered that the Gardens have now been brought in direct touch by rail with nearly all parts of the city, which, in itself, will prove a great boon to the citizens.

The Gardens are bounded on the south by the Great Western Road, which extends, in a straight line, from the Normal School to Anniesland Toll,—a distance of about three miles. From the Botanic Gardens westwards it forms a magnificent promenade for the citizens of the West-End, and there are few cities in the kingdom which can show such a stretch of splendid terraces and handsome mansion-houses.

The Gardens are bounded on the north and west by the suburb of Kelvinside, which takes its name from the old residence of that name. The property was originally a very extensive one, and extended on both sides of the Great Western Road from the Botanic Gardens to Anniesland Toll. It was purchased by Messrs. Montgomerie & Fleming in 1839, and most of it is now laid out for feuing purposes. The mansion-house was situated on the north bank of the river, on the present site of Derby Crescent, but was pulled down several years ago to make way for the extension of the city. North Woodside was another large residential property on the banks of the Kelvin, immediately below the Gardens, which, so far back as 1693, belonged to Robert Campbell, merchant in Glasgow, the ancestor of the Campbells of Blythswood; but it also has disappeared.

The Gardens are bounded on the east by North Park. This property originally belonged to John Hamilton, who was thrice Lord Provost of the city. The original house, which stood behind the present site of Buckingham Terrace and was erected about the beginning of the present century, had extensive gardens and grounds attached to it. The late Mr. John Bell afterwards acquired the property, and erected a handsome residence upon it, which, after his death, was sold, and afterwards became Queen Margaret College, chiefly owing to the liberality of Mrs. John Elder. Now, as is well known, it is affiliated with the University. Within the grounds are two magnificent purple beeches, and a very handsome specimen of the tulip tree.

In connection with the north bank of the Kelvin, opposite the Botanic Gardens, Macdonald, in his *Rambles Round Glasgow*, relates that, in 1769, a young naval lieutenant, George Spearing, whilst gathering nuts on the estate of North Woodside, fell into an old disused pit fifty-one feet deep, where he remained for more than seven days before he was rescued. The place where this incident occurred is immediately to the north of the Flint Mill, where Doune Terrace now stands.

Having thus briefly traced the origin and progress of the Botanic Gardens from being a collection of medicinal plants, or Physic Garden, in connection with the old College in the High Street, to its present position on the banks of the Kelvin, it may be of interest to put on record the several curators who so ably aided in building up, from such small beginnings, a garden and collection of plants which at present stand very high in the horticultural world. Mr. Stewart Murray was the first curator. Previously he had been gardener to Mr. Hopkirk at Dalbeath, and laid out the first gardens in Sauchiehall Street, which were afterwards removed by him to their present site. Mr. Murray was curator for thirty-five years, and was succeeded by Mr. Peter Clark, who held office for sixteen years. Then followed Mr. Robert Bullen, who worthily filled the position for twenty-four years; and all these three gentlemen had hard and uphill work to keep up the Gardens in an efficient manner. The present curator, Mr. Dewar, (who was appointed after Mr. Bullen's death,) has come to us with excellent credentials from Kew,—the finest botanic garden in the world, and under his skilful management the Gardens ought to, and no doubt will, become a distinct success.

The total area at present is about twenty-eight acres, including the recently-acquired ground on the north side of the Kelvin. The natural wooded bank on the south side is still frequented by many song birds, as the following list will show:—

Sparrow Hawk, *Accipiter nisus*, L.
Tawny Owl, *Strix aluco*, L.—Not recently.
Barn Owl, *Aluco flammeus*, L.—Not recently.
Spotted Flycatcher, *Muscicapa grisola*, L.
Mistletoe Thrush, *Turdus viscivorus*, L.
Song Thrush, *Turdus musicus*, L.
Blackbird, *Turdus merula*, L.
Redbreast, *Erithacus rubecula*, L.
Redstart, *Ruticilla phœnicurus*, L.
Stonechat, *Saxicola rubicola*, L.
Greater Whitethroat, *Sylvia rufa*, Bodd.
Garden Warbler, *Sylvia salicaria*, L.
Blackcap, *Sylvia atricapilla*, L.
Wood Warbler, *Phylloscopus sibilatrix*, Bech.
Chiffchaff, *Phylloscopus collybita*, Vieill.

Wren, *Troglodytes parvulus*, K. L. Koch.
Treecreeper, *Certhia familiaris*, L.
Great Titmouse, *Parus major*, L.
Blue Titmouse, *Parus caruleus*, L.
Coal Titmouse, *Parus ater*, L.
Pied Wagtail, *Motacilla lugubris*, Temm.
Yellow Wagtail, *Motacilla raii*, Bonap.
Tree Pipit, *Anthus trivialis*, L.—Not recently.
Meadow Pipit, *Anthus pratensis*, L.
Skylark, *Alauda arvensis*, L.—Not recently.
Reed Bunting, *Emberiza schœniclus*, L.
Common Bunting, *Emberiza miliaria*, L.
Yellow Bunting, *Emberiza citrinella*, L.
Chaffinch, *Fringilla cœlebs*, L.
House Sparrow, *Passer domesticus*, L.
Greenfinch, *Coccothraustes chloris*, L.
Goldfinch, *Carduelis elegans*, Steph.—Occasionally.
Linnet, *Linota cannabina*, L.
Bullfinch, *Pyrrhula europea*, Vieill.
Starling, *Sturnus vulgaris*, L.
Rook, *Corvus frugilegus*, L.
Jackdaw, *Corvus monedula*, L.
The Pie, *Pica rustica*, Scopoli.
Swallow, *Hirundo rustica*, L.
Cuckow, *Cuculus canorus*, L.—Occasionally.
Wood Pigeon, *Columba palumbus*, L.
Pheasant, *Phasianus colchicus*, L.—Occasionally.
Partridge, *Perdix cinerea*, Lath.—Occasionally. Probably from Garscube.
Lapwing, *Vanellus vulgaris*, Bech.
Black-headed Gull, *Larus ridibundus*, L.

A number of crows took up their quarters, several years ago, in the large trees near Queen Margaret College, and they are yearly increasing in numbers. In 1893 there were ninety nests. Both the crows and birds should be carefully protected by the public, as they lend a special charm to this rural retreat.

On the south bank of the Kelvin there is one landmark which must be well known to many Glasgow citizens, and which has recently wellnigh disappeared. Twenty years ago the Pear Tree Well, or Three Tree Well, was a favourite spot for picnics for the younger generation. It was situated immediately opposite the flat plateau at the bend of the river above the Gardens. The well itself has now ceased to exist, but there are three trees, two ash and one plane, which still mark the spot.

During the summer the Gardens are largely taken advantage of, 12,000 persons having visited them on a fine Sunday in August. Musical performances were also given from May till October,—the average attendance at the concerts being between 5,000 and 6,000 persons.

VII.

MAXWELL PARK.

MAXWELL PARK is situated to the south-west of Pollokshields, one of the largest and most rising suburbs of Glasgow. It was presented to the burgh by Sir John Stirling-Maxwell, Bart., in 1878, as a place of recreation and amusement for his feuars. The area is about 20 acres, and it consists principally of flat moss land.

The Commissioners of Pollokshields lost no time in laying out the park, and commenced by enclosing it with a light railing of handsome and ornamental design. As the situation is somewhat low and rather damp, and the soil very moist, owing to its mossy character, a thorough system of drainage was carried out, whereby both the spring and the surface water was conveyed to the lowest point in the park. Here an ornamental lake or pond was formed, which is used during the spring and summer months for the sailing of model yachts, and during the winter months as a skating pond for the children of

Mazur – Park

Pollokshields and the immediate vicinity. Roads and walks were formed, and a belting of trees and shrubs was also planted, as well as several avenues of trees. At considerable expense the Commissioners erected at the south-east corner of the park a commodious Burgh Hall, which is both useful and ornamental, and is now a great boon to the whole locality.

Consequent upon the extension of the city in 1891, East and West Pollokshields were included in Greater Glasgow, along with the Maxwell Park. Considerable alterations and improvements have since then been carried out by the Corporation. A handsome bandstand has been erected, as well as drinking fountains, waiting-rooms, &c. The belting of trees and shrubs round the park has been re-arranged, so as to allow visitors a view of the villas in the vicinity, with their ornamental pleasure-grounds. A plot near the main entrance has been laid off as an American flower garden, planted principally with plants which are at home in a peaty soil, such as rhododendrons, azaleas, kalmias, menezias, acubas, heaths, &c. There are other parts of the park to which with advantage this arrangement might be extended, as, when once formed, the plants require little or no attention. Owing to the limited area of the park and the nature of the ground, the park is not well suited for football and cricket, but with careful top-dressing of good soil, it could easily be made available for lawn tennis and similar games.

The only mansion-houses of note in the vicinity are Haggs Castle and Pollok House, both belonging to Sir John Stirling-Maxwell. The former, Haggs Castle, is situated a short distance to the west of the park, and is an old baronial mansion, built in 1585 by one of Sir John's ancestors. Its walls are upwards of five feet thick, and it is reported to be the last of four castles built upon various sites by this family. About the middle of last century it was allowed to fall into disrepair, but several years ago it was restored by the late Sir John Maxwell, and is now the residence of Mr. Thomas College, the resident factor and agent for the estate, which extends for several miles north-west and south from this point.

Pollok House, which is Sir John Stirling-Maxwell's present residence, was built in 1752, and is situated upon the banks of the Cart, about two miles west of the park. It is surrounded by extensive pleasure-grounds, richly wooded with grand old timber, which, however, suffered severely from the storm of November, 1893, which devastated the country. In particular, two large wych elms, known as the Renfrewshire elms, were laid low. These magnificent trees were 90 feet high and 13 feet 9 inches in circumference, and were supposed to be over 300 years old. In the courtyard of the stables adjoining the gardens there is to be seen a very fine specimen of the *Ampelopsis hederacea*, or Virginian creeper. From one root it extends along two sides of the yard a distance of 310 feet, and covers 344 square yards of wall. Sir John Stirling-Maxwell allows visitors to his grounds during the summer months on Saturdays, from 2 o'clock to 7 o'clock.

With regard to the laying out of the burgh of Pollokshields, Sir John Stirling-Maxwell and his predecessor, along with their advisers, are to be congratulated upon the liberal manner in which it has been carried out. Forty years ago it was entirely agricultural land, and the villas now cover an area of between 300 and 400 acres, in holdings of from a-quarter of an acre to one acre. The streets and drives are wide and spacious, the drainage is perfect, and open spaces and playgrounds have been provided for children, thus making it, in every respect, a model suburb.

With reference to the peaty or mossy character of the soil of the Maxwell Park, it is worth noting that the whole area, along with a considerable extent of the adjoining lands, must have been at one time a forest of large trees, principally oak. When digging out the drains and the lake many stems and roots were found, some of them five feet deep in the moss, and with the bark adhering. Specimens may be seen at a rockery near the lake. The names of Haggs Castle and Haggs Bows Farm in the neighbourhood point to the fact that the whole must have been covered with water and vegetation at one time,—so as to form the Moss Haggs.

A census of the visitors to the park was taken on 13th August, 1893, when 9500 persons entered the park by the various gates between 6 A.M. and 10 P.M. Musical performances were given during the summer months, with an average attendance of 670 persons.

VIII.

SPRINGBURN AND RUCHILL PARKS.

THESE parks have been recently acquired by the Corporation as recreation grounds for the northern outlying districts of the city, and they are both at present (1894) in course of being laid out.

Springburn Park is situated upon rising ground to the north of what was known, till a few years ago, as a small country village of that name. Owing, however, to the extension of railways and the erection of public works in its vicinity, it is now a large manufacturing district, with a population of about 23,000. Possilpark, another large industrial centre, is distant about a mile due west, and has a population of about 11,000.

The park contains about 56 acres of undulating ground, and was formerly known as Mosesfield and Cock Muir. It was purchased in 1892, and plans were at once prepared by the city engineer, showing how it could be laid out, both with the view of providing a suitable recreation ground, and also of utilizing the margin of the park, in certain places, for feuing purposes, as in several of the other parks.

Operations were shortly afterwards commenced to lay it out by draining, ploughing, and road-making; and considerable progress was made in 1893 in this direction. There is, therefore, now a large area of it in green sward, and planting operations are being pushed forward, so that the park is in fairly good order. A large pond has been formed for sailing model yachts, and a handsome bandstand has been added, which was opened in May, 1893. Musical performances were given once a-week during the summer months, the average attendance being 2680.

The view from the highest point in the park, which is 350 feet above the level of the sea, is both varied and grand. To the north there can be seen Ben Lomond, and the neighbouring hills around Loch Katrine and the Trossachs, whilst to the east lie part of the Ochils and the Kilsyth range. To the west Goatfell is visible, in the distance, on a clear day, and, nearer at hand, the Argyllshire hills above Dunoon, and the Kilpatrick and Campsie ranges; whilst in the immediate foreground are the richly-wooded Blane and Kelvin Valleys, with numerous residential mansion-houses.

Ruchill Park is situated about two miles to the west of Springburn Park, and stands about the same elevation above the sea level. It comprises 53 acres of undulating ground, and is bounded on the south and west by the Monkland Canal. On the north there is a new road, or street, running from the Maryhill Road to Possil Park; and on the east the Health Committee have acquired ground for an hospital, which is to be on much the same lines as Belvidere in the east end of the city.

The park derives its name from the old house and estate of Ruchill. The original house was built about the year 1700, but since then considerable additions have been made to it. It is situated a short distance north of the park, surrounded by grand old trees, and was long occupied by several well-known Glasgow families, such as the Peddies, Dreghorns, and Davidsons. The park was purchased from the present representative of the last-named family, Mr. W. J. Davidson, in 1892, and is now in course of being laid out, along with Springburn Park, under the able superintendence of Mr. James Whitton, the recently-appointed curator of public parks.

Ruchill Park, when finished, will prove an immense boon to the large industrial classes of Possil Park, Cowcaddens, Kelvinside, and Maryhill, and it is worthy of consideration whether a golf course could not be arranged in the park. The ground appears to be suitable, and it would, doubtless, be largely taken advantage of.

The views from this park are very similar to those from Springburn Park, especially to the west and north. The foreground, however, is much superior, looking down over the richly-wooded policies of Garscube and Killermont, which have been both carefully planted for landscape effect.

A field of about 5½ acres was purchased in 1893 by the Corporation at the north end of Maryhill, and laid out as a place of amusement and recreation for children, with a rustic place of shelter. It has proved of great benefit to the Maryhill district, and is much appreciated.

IX.

PUBLIC SQUARES, OPEN SPACES, AND RECREATION GROUNDS.

ABOUT the beginning of this century, and while Glasgow was still of moderate dimensions, open spaces were not so urgently required as they are at the present time. The city had not then stretched its mighty arms in every direction, and the property speculator was unknown. Without much trouble or expense, or loss of time, the inhabitants could, if they desired it, avail themselves of the green fields and all the beauties of nature. The Glasgow Green was then the only public park within the boundaries of the city, and, as rank and fashion had not migrated to the West-End, it was the general recreation ground for all classes of the community. As the city increased, however, in extent and in wealth, the richer merchants erected larger and more substantial houses, either in the centre of private pleasure-grounds, or in the immediate vicinity of some square or public garden. Amongst the latter may be mentioned George Square, St. Enoch Square, St. Andrew Square, and Grafton Square, which all still remain as open spaces to the public. Year by year the city continued to increase in size, especially westwards; and, in the case of residences for the wealthier classes, provision was frequently made for improving the character and outlook of the houses by the acquisition of a private pleasure-ground for the use of their inhabitants. Examples of these private grounds are to be found in Blythswood Square, Elmbank Crescent, Queen's Crescent, Woodside Crescent, Claremont Terrace, Park Circus, &c., &c. The same system has been carried out in most of the outlying suburbs of the city, and has proved of immense value to the upper classes.

The present chapter, however, is intended to deal with what has been done in the way of providing open spaces for the general public, and to direct attention to the great good which is being done by the Corporation in a very quiet way. In 1859 the Glasgow Public Parks Act was passed, under which powers were obtained to acquire lands for the purpose of forming public parks, and for levying assessments for their upkeep, but no provision was made for open spaces in contradistinction to parks. This was remedied, however, by the City Improvement Acts of 1866 and subsequent years, which, *inter alia*, empowered the Corporation to open up and improve the congested parts of the city by forming wider streets, and providing recreation grounds and public squares. In this way the City and Streets Improvement Committee acquired and laid out many open spaces, such as Overnewton, Oatlands, and Cathedral Squares. Another example of the useful work which this Committee executed is to be found in the excellent arrangement of the ground to the north of Kelvingrove Park, near to Woodlands Road and Blythswood Drive, which otherwise would have been built upon. A further step towards providing open spaces was taken by the Corporation in 1878, when they acquired powers from Parliament for taking over the disused churchyards or burying grounds. In this way the Corporation have obtained the control of, and laid out, six churchyards—the most important of which is the Ramshorn.

George Square, which is the oldest and also the most important of the public squares, contains an area of about two acres. It is the property of the city, and forms part of the "Ramshorn Croft," which was purchased by the Corporation from Hutchesons' Hospital about the year 1772, and the other portions of which have all been sold or feued. About 1778, building operations were going on in the immediate vicinity, and the present site of the square, which was then a waste hollow, usually filled with stagnant water, was utilized as a place for depositing the earth and sand excavated from the foundations. A wooden paling was erected round the enclosure, and the only use made of it was for the grazing of cattle. As time advanced, and the square became a place of considerable importance, the Corporation considered that something should be done towards improving it; and, accordingly, in 1825, Mr. Stewart Murray, then curator of the Botanic Gardens, was instructed to have it laid out. The old paling was removed, and a substantial iron railing erected in its place. Winding walks were formed, and trees and shrubs planted. At that time the only statue in the square was that of Sir John Moore.

For many years thereafter the square was kept up by the hotel-keepers and others who resided in it. The late Bailie Whyte, who lived at the south-west corner, took charge of it, and collected the subscriptions. It was not, at that time, open to the public, and keys were, with some few exceptions, given only to the residenters in the square. It was, however, occasionally used for flower shows, which were held in tents.

Matters continued very much in this position till 1862, when the Corporation took the square under their own management, and improved it very considerably. It had come to be recognised as the most suitable situation for statues erected to public men, and the condition in which it had been kept had not been satisfactory. The residenters in the square, about this time, endeavoured to assert that it was their property, but the claim was departed from.

When the new Post Office was built, in 1876, and when the entire square was boarded over for the laying of the foundation-stone by the Prince of Wales, a new arrangement of the plots was made. The railing round the square was removed, transverse walks were formed, and it assumed very much the appearance which it now has. Flower beds were formed, which have proved remarkably successful.

There is, probably, no park or open space in the city which comes so prominently before the public as George Square, and neither money nor trouble should be spared in making it as attractive as possible at all seasons of the year. There is nothing more refreshing to the eye than a sward of beautiful grass, and for some years past this has been one of the features of the square. In one respect, however, its general appearance might be improved. The railing which at present encloses the plots, whilst fulfilling its purpose, is far from ornamental. A substantial and handsome railing, three feet high, upon a stone base of about one foot six inches, similar to that around the ornamental plots in front of the Parliament Houses in London, would give a character to the square, and would also be more in keeping with the many artistic statues and handsome public buildings which now adorn it. There is also a suggestion which had the approval of the late Mr. John Carrick, and which should not be lost sight of. It is, that the base of Sir Walter Scott's Monument should be encircled by Loch Katrine water. Nothing could be more appropriate or more effective.

St. Andrew Square and St. Enoch Square, which are now both paved over, were at one time surrounded by the residences of wealthy Glasgow citizens. St. Andrew's Church, the building of which was commenced in 1739, and completed in 1758, was surrounded by a churchyard; but the actual building of the square round it did not begin till about the year 1790. For about fifty years afterwards the square was the most fashionable residential locality in the city. St. Enoch Square originally belonged to an old Glasgow family called Luke. It was sold by them to the Merchants' House, and afterwards it was purchased by the Corporation, who resolved to erect one of the city churches on the site. This was accordingly done in 1780. Thereafter the adjoining ground, as in the case of George Square, was either sold or feued, and the centre was laid off in grass, with an iron railing round it, and grazed by sheep. Like St. Andrew Square, it became a favourite locality, chiefly for its quiet and retired character. The grass plot remained in St. Enoch Square till about 1860, when it was removed to make way for the farmers, who, in that year, were prohibited from meeting in Stockwell Street on the Wednesday market-days, and who, thereafter, made St. Enoch Square their place of meeting. They continued to meet there till 1892, when, owing to railway operations in the square, they were again forced to move, much against their inclination, to the Corn Exchange in Hope Street.

Grafton Square is also one of the old city squares, situated to the north of Stirling Road, and it still affords its inhabitants a glimpse of green in the midst of a densely populated centre. It also, in its day, was surrounded by fashionable residences.

In the way of recently-acquired squares and open spaces the City Improvement Trustees began with Overnewton, Oatlands, and Cathedral Squares. These were carefully laid out with walks and seats, and planted with trees, shrubs, and flowers. Messrs. M'Dowall, Steven & Co. presented Cathedral Square with a handsome fountain, which plays on fine days during the summer months, and is a great source of pleasure to the inhabitants in the vicinity.

Hutcheson Square—the area of which is about three-quarters of an acre—was presented to the city by the preceptor and patrons of Hutchesons' Hospital in the year 1888. It is situated in the centre of their densely-populated property on the south-side of the river; and one half of it has been laid off with grass, flowers, shrubs, and trees,—the remaining half being left as a playground for children. There is also a drinking fountain in the centre of the square, and seats have been placed round it.

Maxwell Square, in East Pollokshields, is of similar dimensions to Hutcheson Square, and has been laid out in the same style. It may be looked upon as a model of what a children's playground ought to be.

There is a square of nearly four acres at Govanhill, and also a smaller one of two acres at Titwood (the latter being the gift of Sir John Stirling Maxwell), both of which are at present (1894) in course of formation.

The Phœnix Recreation Ground, situated at the junction of New City Road and Garscube Road, is worthy of special notice. Its site was formerly that of the Phœnix Foundry—one of the oldest-established ironworks in the city. It consists of about three acres; and was purchased,

Cathedral Square.

Phœnix Square.

about two years ago, by the Public Health Committee for £25,000. It was laid out and fully equipped by them, both for pleasure and amusement, with trees, flowers, shrubs, seats, and gymnasium. The last-mentioned has two divisions,—one for boys and the other for girls,—with a competent caretaker in charge, to maintain order and prevent accidents as much as possible. Messrs. Buchanan Brothers presented a large and ornamental fountain, and the Public Health Committee have provided a bandstand and drinking fountain. As this locality of the Cowcaddens is one of the most crowded and congested in any part of the city, the opening of this playground must be an immense boon to the inhabitants in the neighbourhood.

With regard to the disused churchyards which have been brought under the charge of the Parks Committee and maintained by them as open spaces for the benefit of the public, the Ramshorn, or St. David's, in Ingram Street, was the first taken in hand. It consists of about one-and-a-half acres, and was opened to the public in 1879. Walks were formed, trees and shrubs planted, and the walls and monuments repaired. The memorial tablets or stones were adjusted, the upright stones being generally laid flat. All the old iron guards which had been erected round the lairs in the time of the "Resurrection Scare," and which were unclaimed, were removed and sold for old iron, the sum received nearly covering the cost of the improvements. About the same time the churchyards in Clyde Street (Calton), John Street (Bridgeton), North Street, and Clyde Street (Anderston), were taken over; and a few years later the old Gorbals burying ground, containing upwards of two acres, was also included. These have all been laid out in the same way as the Ramshorn Churchyard, and are open to the public from 10 a.m. to 8 p.m. during the summer months, and from 10 a.m. till dusk during the remainder of the year. The opening up of these churchyards has been of immense benefit, in providing a breathing space for the inhabitants in their immediate vicinity,—especially in the way of affording an opportunity for quiet out-door exercise for aged people and invalids, who are not able to travel as far as the public parks. They are always kept in excellent order, and, in the summer time, when the grass is green and the flowers are in bloom, they form pleasant retreats from the bustle and hurry of our noisy streets. There are several other churchyards in the city which could be utilized in the same way, and no doubt our authorities will turn their attention to them at the proper time.

The following is a list of the squares, open spaces, and churchyards which are now under the supervision of the

Parks Committee, and are maintained by them out of the public rates:—

	AREA.		
	A.	R.	P.
George Square,	2	0	0
Oatlands Square,	0	2	16
Hutcheson Square,	0	3	24
Cathedral Square,	1	1	24
Phœnix Square,	2	1	24
Overnewton Square,	0	2	16
Maxwell Square,	0	3	24
Clydeside,	0	3	24
Pollok Street,	0	1	32
Blythswood Drive,	0	1	24
Wishart Street,	0	2	16
Gorbals Churchyard,	2	1	24
Ramshorn Churchyard,	1	2	0
North Street Churchyard,	1	0	0
Clyde Street (Anderston) Churchyard,	0	2	0
Clyde Street (Calton) Churchyard,	1	1	8
John Street (Calton) Churchyard,	1	0	32
High Churchyard,	4	0	0
Ground at Govanhill,	4	0	0
Ground at Titwood,	2	0	0
Total acreage,	29	0	8

From the foregoing short account of the squares and open spaces in the city, it will be seen that the Corporation, almost from the very first, have recognised their usefulness, and in later years have been steadily advancing in the right direction towards increasing their number and importance. It is to be hoped that they will continue to do so, especially in the way of providing playgrounds for children, many of whom can have but few opportunities of going to the public parks for recreation and amusement.

In this connection it is interesting to note what is being done in this direction in London. In that city it has been left to private philanthropy to accomplish what is being done in Glasgow by the public authorities. In 1882 the Metropolitan Public Gardens Association was formed, with the object of securing available plots of ground, large or small, and of obtaining the right of laying out and planting all disused burying grounds, enclosed squares, &c. These were to be utilized as gardens or as playgrounds, the latter to be watched over by a caretaker, who, during certain hours, would be able to instruct the children in simple gymnastics. The Association has also amongst its objects the opening of every school playground to the children of the neighbourhood at all suitable hours. The success which has attended the Association may be gathered from the following extract from its annual report for 1893:—

"Fifty-nine gardens and twenty playgrounds, (exclusive "of school playgrounds,) covering an area of 94 acres, "have in eleven years, at a cost of nearly £30,000, been "added to the open spaces of London, through the instru- "mentality of the Association, excluding numerous grounds "towards the improvement of which the Association has

"contributed. In addition, some 2500 trees have been
"planted in the thoroughfares, and about 1200 seats placed
"in the streets, and a far greater number in the public
"gardens of the Metropolis."

The work which this Association is carrying out is most laudable, and the success which is attending it, supported, as it is, only by subscription, should stimulate our Corporation and wealthy citizens to increase their efforts in the same direction.

X.

THE ELDER PARK, GOVAN.

THIS Park was presented to the burgh of Govan by Mrs. John Elder, in affectionate remembrance of her husband, and of his father, David Elder,—the former of whom was long connected with the famous firm of Randolph, Elder & Co., now known as the Fairfield Shipbuilding Company. This act of generosity on the part of that lady is the first example of a private individual presenting a public park to the City of Glasgow or any of its suburbs,—an example which has since been followed by more than one of our citizens.

The park contains about 37 acres and is situated immediately to the south of the Fairfield Works, with a frontage to the Renfrew Road of 1550 feet. The surface is almost flat, and, as the soil and sub-soil are of a sandy nature and thus do not long retain moisture, it is admirably suited for a public park or recreation ground for an industrial community such as Govan.

The ground was acquired by Mrs. Elder in 1883, and

"The Elder Park, Govan"

the actual work of laying it out was commenced in the spring of the following year. All the details in connection with it received Mrs. Elder's personal supervision, and no expense was spared to make it complete in every respect. The park was completed towards the middle of 1885, and the formal ceremony of handing it over to the authorities of the burgh of Govan was performed by the Earl of Rosebery on the 27th of June in the same year, the day being held as a public holiday in Govan.

The method adopted in the laying-out of the ground was by the formation of a gracefully-curved carriage drive, 20 feet wide, all round the park, leaving the centre portion available for recreation purposes. A strong artistic iron railing encloses the whole grounds, and the main entrance, which is from Renfrew Road and almost at the north-east corner of the park, is specially handsome. It consists of six massive stone pillars, with ornamental iron gates, the two pillars in the centre being furnished with handsomely carved standards and ornamental lamps. At the south-east corner of the park an entrance has been provided from Langlands Road, and also from the west, at Holmfauldhead Road.

The planting of the park was carried out in the most liberal way by the generous donor. The only trees upon the property, when it was converted into a park, were a few large elms along the Renfrew Road. A broad belting of trees and shrubbery was, however, planted round the park immediately inside the railing, and numerous clumps of trees and beds of rhododendrons and other evergreen shrubs were planted in several parts. No expense was spared in the selection of suitable trees and shrubs for immediate as well as permanent effect, and the result has been most successful. The young plants, which were planted about twelve years ago, have made remarkable progress, and a judicious thinning out, especially of the soft-wooded, fast-growing varieties, which were only put in for immediate effect, would enable the permanent trees and shrubs to attain their proper size and proportions, and at the same time the undergrowth would be properly developed. The shrubs have all done remarkably well, especially the elders, which seem to be well suited for the soil and to be striving to do credit to the honoured name which the park bears.

The flower garden is situated towards the south-west corner of the park, and it has been specially laid out with the object of being attractive both in summer and winter. In our variable climate too much attention cannot be given to plants which are of interest all the year round, and especially to spring flowers.

The central portion of the park, as already stated, is

devoted to the purposes of recreation and amusement. It is divided into two portions by a broad walk or promenade running from north to south, and in the centre there is a bandstand. With regard to recreation purposes, Mrs. Elder, in gifting the park, made it a special stipulation that no games, such as cricket or football, should be allowed. Whilst this may seem a somewhat hard regulation to many of the rising generation in Govan, it is a wise provision, because these games, although beneficial to a section of the community, are, at the same time, objectionable and even dangerous to the most of the frequenters of the park.

The bandstand, which was also erected by Mrs. Elder, is situated almost in the centre of the park. It is octagonal in shape, and the design has been much admired. Overhead there is an ornamental canopy of metal, which is well suited as a sounding board for the musical performances. The canopy is supported by eight carved pillars. The dado round the base of the stand is most artistic. It consists of panels illustrative of shipbuilding, music, and art, and in the south panel there has been inserted a plate, giving the name of the donor of the park, and the object for which it was given. Since the park was opened a raised platform of oval shape has been constructed immediately to the west of the bandstand. This has also been erected by Mrs. Elder, and is for the purpose of accommodating the pipe band of the Govan Police, organized by Captain Hamilton, the superintendent of the Govan Police force. Evergreens and flowers have been planted round the bandstand and the pipers' platform, and in this way the somewhat bare appearance of the centre of the park has been much relieved.

In laying out the park Mrs. Elder has not forgotten the wants of a shipbuilding community such as Govan. A pond has been formed, 380 feet long and 165 feet broad, which has been specially constructed for the sailing of model yachts. In the centre it is two feet six inches deep, and it shallows towards the sides. It is formed of two separate layers of concrete, with a thin sheet of bitumen between them; and no difficulty has been experienced in keeping the pond watertight.

The arrangements made for carrying on the work of the park are very complete. The old farm-house on the ground has been altered and improved into a superintendent's house, with suitable waiting-rooms for the public attached to it. Immediately behind it are the necessary offices, comprising plant-houses, tool-houses, &c. A flagstaff, 105 feet high, has also been erected in a prominent position in the park.

In 1887 the working men of Govan resolved that some recognition should be made of Mr. John Elder's ability, and of his close connections with the prosperity of the burgh, and it was agreed that a statue in the park was the most appropriate form which the testimonial could take. There was no lack of subscriptions, and the commission was placed in the hands of Sir J. E. Boehm. The statue was erected in the eastern section of the park, immediately opposite the main entrance. It was unveiled by the Marquis of Lothian, the Secretary of State for Scotland, on 28th July, 1888, and is not only a faithful likeness, but is also a work of art and an ornament to the park.

It has been already mentioned that Mrs. Elder, in gifting the park, made special provision for the prohibition of all games, and at the same time it was stipulated that it should be possessed "principally for "the use and enjoyment of the inhabitants in the way "of healthful recreation by music and amusements." Concerts are regularly given in the bandstands during nearly six months of the year, and the attendance at them proves that the intentions of the donor have been fully realized.

It is interesting to note that the site now occupied by the Elder Park forms part of the original riverside estate of Fairfield,—a portion of which was purchased by Messrs. Randolph, Elder & Co., in 1863, for their shipbuilding yard. The park proper is really a portion of Fairfield Farm or estate, which was for many years occupied by Mr. Alexander Thomson; and, from the fertile nature of the soil, one is not surprised to hear that it was considered a model farm. Fairfield House is still in existence, and is used by the Fairfield Shipbuilding Company as part of their offices.

Immediately to the west of the park was the estate and mansion-house of Linthouse, occupied in turn by the well-known Glasgow families of Watsons and Rowans. The mansion-house still remains, and occupies a central position in the shipbuilding yard of Messrs. Alexander Stephen & Sons. To the south of the park is the fine old residence of Moor Park, which now belongs to the Glasgow and South-Western Railway Company. It was originally the property of the Oswalds of Shieldhall, and was for a long period the residence of Bailie John Mitchell, a most respected citizen of Glasgow in the first half of this century. To the east of the park was the estate of Cessnock. The mansion-house was built in 1800, when the property belonged to the Hunters, who were well-known Glasgow merchants. It was afterwards occupied by Bailie Fowler as a nursery, which has now disappeared, but the name is still retained in the Cessnock Dock, which is situated on the property.

The progress which has been made by the burgh of Govan is most remarkable. In 1864 the population was only 9,000; in 1893 it was over 63,000. To shipbuilding enterprise this increase is almost entirely due, and it is therefore most appropriate that the park which has been presented to the burgh should be commemorative of one who did so much towards founding its prosperity.

XI.

VICTORIA PARK, PARTICK.

THIS park, extending to about forty-six acres of undulating land, was feued from Mr. J. Gordon Oswald of Scotstoun in 1886, the terms being £5 per acre per annum for ten years and £10 per acre thereafter in perpetuity, these terms being about one-sixth of the usual feuing rates on the estate. Since then Mr. Gordon Oswald has, in a very generous manner, spontaneously discharged the increased feu-duty and fixed the perpetual feu-duty at £5 per acre, which means a gift of nearly £6000 to the burgh of Partick. The work of laying-out was commenced in November, 1886, when there was unusual depression in the shipbuilding trade, and large numbers of operatives were going about idle and almost in starvation. The scheme was suggested by the burgh authorities, chiefly to give work to the unemployed, and in connection with it nearly £4000 was spent in wages. The park was formally opened on Saturday, 2nd July, 1887, by Provost Sir Andrew M'Lean, and was, with the

The Victoria Park, Purlock.

consent of the Queen, named the Victoria Park, in honour of her Majesty's jubilee.

The park is bounded on the east by Balshagray Avenue, and extends due west, almost parallel to the Dumbarton Road, for a distance of 880 yards. There are four entrance gates at various points, the principal one being from Balshagray Avenue. There is a spacious carriage drive all round the park, 24 feet wide, in graceful curves. It is about a mile in length, and there are also upwards of two miles of walks. A belting of trees and shrubs surrounds the park, and there are numerous plots of flowers and rhododendrons in various parts. Advantage has been taken of the lowest parts to form an ornamental lake, of about four acres in extent, for the sailing of model yachts, and also for skating in winter; and it forms one of the principal features of the park. The water is supplied from springs in the neighbourhood. There is also a smaller lake, which has an island specially constructed for the protection and breeding of fancy water-fowl. A handsome flagpole, 90 feet high, with shelter round the base, 22 feet in diameter, was erected at the highest point by the late ex-Provost Ferguson, who deserves the chief credit both for the purchase and for the laying-out of the park. Unfortunately, he did not live to see the result of his labours, as he died very shortly before it was opened.

Near to Balshagray Avenue spaces have been let to Partick clubs at nominal rents, for the purposes of lawn tennis and curling. It is proposed to add about sixteen acres on the north side of the park, and in this way additional recreation ground will be provided. A band performs in the park during the summer months. The park is well furnished with seats, drinking-fountains, waiting-rooms, and tool and plant houses. The ladies of Partick deserve a special notice for their gift of the handsome ornamental gates with pillars at Balshagray Avenue, upon which there is a suitable inscription to commemorate the jubilee year of the Queen. Mr. Gordon Oswald of Scotstoun presented an artistic clock, which has been erected on an elevated floral mound in proximity to the lake, and it is both ornamental and useful.

The most interesting part of the Victoria Park, from a natural history and geological point of view, is the Quarry Knowe, elevated some 55 feet above the sea level, and upon which there is a handsome group of large beech, plane, and elm trees. The knowe is composed of whinstone rock, and has been, for a long period, utilized as a quarry, principally for the purpose of obtaining metal for the repairing of roads. In 1887, when the workmen forming the park were cutting a walk through the strata of sandstone and shale which lay along the bottom of this old quarry, they discovered ten fossil stems and roots of trees in the exact position in which they grew thousands of years ago, all within an area of 280 square yards, and at a depth of about 40 feet from the top of the knowe. Several examples of similar fossil trees have been found in quarries around Glasgow, specially at Gilmorehill and Kelvingrove Park; but this discovery at the Victoria Park is considered the most important which has been made in the West of Scotland, and is specially valuable on account of the limited area in which it is situated. The Partick authorities have erected a covering over this fossil grove. It consists of a substantial erection of brick, wood, and glass, 75 feet long by 34 feet broad, constructed so as to protect these unique specimens of a long past vegetation. The structure is well suited for the purpose of protecting the fossils from the effects of the weather. It is, however, capable of improvement by covering the walls, both externally and internally, with vegetation of the present day, such as Scotch ivies, *ampelopsis*, and *ficus*. It might be advisable to have a hot-water pipe under the gangway which has been so judiciously constructed a few feet above the grove; and this would not only protect the fossils in frosty weather, but also benefit the tree-ferns and other plants in the fossil-house. It may be noted that several varieties of ferns are springing up spontaneously from the fissures of the sandstone shale, which may prove to be types of the older flora of the country.

This fossil grove has attracted the attention of scientists and geologists from all parts of the country. Two of our well-known geologists, Dr. John Young and the late Mr. D. C. Glen, published an interesting pamphlet upon the subject, and have also compiled a leaflet as to details, which is posted up in the fossil house. There are to be seen in the house, on a table over the fossil grove, several cinerary urns belonging to the later Stone Period. These were found when levelling a portion of the top of the knowe, near where the trees are seen. One of the urns is perfect, and in it, and in close proximity to it, were found a quantity of calcined human bones, and also a small beautifully-formed stone hammer, polished on its surface and ornamented. This would seem to indicate that the knowe formed a place of interment during the Stone Period, and probably before the last rise of the land in Scotland, when the eminence would be an island. The date of the urns has been fixed by scientists at about 1000 B.C., and this find of human remains shows that cremation was used in olden times to decompose the dead.

Bailie Storrie of Whiteinch, and Mr. Duncan, curator of the park, deserve every credit for the discovery of the fossils, urns, and human remains, and also for the planting and general laying-out of the park, especially in the way of aiding nature in the neighbourhood of the old quarry by judicious planting.

There are several places of interest in the neighbourhood. Scotstoun House, with its property of 1000 acres, has been in the possession of the Oswald family since 1751, and is now a most valuable estate for feuing purposes. Jordanhill, another well-known property, immediately to the north of the park, has been owned by the Smith family since 1800. The late Mr. James Smith was well known as an antiquarian, and as one of the most learned gentlemen of his generation. The house was built in 1782, and commands an extensive view of the Vale of Clyde. The home park is large, and richly wooded.

In the immediate vicinity of the park there have been recently erected several ranges of small self-contained houses, the best examples of the kind in the neighbourhood of Glasgow. There are garden plots attached to each house, and, from the neat and attractive manner in which they are kept, the locality is worthy of attention as containing models of cottage homes for the middle classes, which, in many cases, are owned by the occupants. With the facilities now afforded by our new railway systems, proprietors in the suburbs might well follow the example of the Scotstoun estate, and dispose of their property at moderate rates and in a similar manner. In this way they would afford an opportunity to many industrious citizens of becoming proprietors of their own cottage homes, and, at the same time, make their properties more attractive from a picturesque point of view. It is worthy of note that the streets have been liberally treated by Mr. Gordon Oswald, and have been planted with avenues of suitable shade trees, which, in the course of time, will give quite a character to this interesting little suburb of Partick.

From the foregoing notes it will be seen that the Victoria Park is well suited for an industrial community such as Partick, which has increased very rapidly during the last thirty years. In 1864 the population was only about 10,000, and now it is nearly 45,000. The authorities of the burgh deserve every credit for having secured this beautiful park as a place of amusement, recreation, and instruction for the inhabitants of Partick for all time coming.

APPENDIX I.

STATEMENTS SHEWING ORDINARY REVENUE AND EXPENDITURE FOR THE UPKEEP OF THE GLASGOW PUBLIC PARKS, ART GALLERIES, AND MUSEUMS, COMPILED FROM STATISTICS SUPPLIED BY THE KINDNESS OF JAMES NICOL, ESQ., CITY CHAMBERLAIN.

1. ORDINARY REVENUE.

Year.	Population.	Rate.	Revenue from Assessment.	Revenue from Feus, Rents, Grazing Rents, &c.	Total Ordinary Revenue.
1861	395,503	2d.	£10,910	£2,413	£13,323
1871	477,732	2d.	15,191	2,019	17,210
1881	511,415	1¾d.	19,312	4,607	23,919
1891	565,714	2d.	24,931	3,311	28,242
1894*	684,148	2½d.	33,566	3,600	37,166

* In 1891 the City Boundaries were extended by the inclusion of several neighbouring Burghs and Districts.

APPENDIX I.—*continued.*

2. ORDINARY EXPENDITURE.

Year.	Parks and Minor Spaces.	Galleries and Museums.	Music.	Interest and Sinking Fund.*	Management and Sundries.	Total Ordinary Expenditure.
1861	£1,020	£555	—	£8,192	£534	£10,301
1871	2,946	1,096	—	8,453	283	12,778
1881	5,662	3,281	£820	12,143	1,080	22,986
1891	8,092	3,728	677	11,413	1,600	25,510
1894	11,997	4,118	1,740	17,453	2,475	37,783

* By Act of Parliament the Corporation of Glasgow are bound to set aside yearly a proportion of the Assessments for the formation of a Sinking Fund to defray the original cost of the various Parks. This Sinking Fund amounted, in 1894, to £64,270 5s. 9d.

APPENDIX II.

LIST OF PUBLIC PARKS AND OPEN SPACES IN THE CITY OF GLASGOW IN 1893.

	A.	R.	P.
Glasgow Green,	136	0	0
Kelvingrove Park,	85	0	0
Queen's Park and Camphill,	148	0	0
Alexandra Park,	94	0	0
Springburn Park,	56	0	0
Ruchill Park,	53	0	0
Cathkin Braes,	49	0	0
Maxwell Park,	20	0	0
Botanic Gardens,	28	0	0
Maryhill Recreation Grounds,	5	2	0
Govanhill Recreation Grounds,	4	0	0
George Square,	2	0	0
Cathedral Square,	1	1	24
Phœnix Square,	2	1	24
Overnewton Square,	0	2	10
Oatlands Square,	0	2	16
Hutcheson Square,	0	3	24
Ramshorn Churchyard,	1	2	0
St. Mark's Churchyard,	0	2	0
Gorbals Churchyard,	2	1	24
Calton Churchyard (Clyde Street),	1	1	8
John Street Churchyard (Calton),	1	0	32
Old Calton Street Churchyard,	0	0	0
High Church Churchyard,	4	0	0
Maxwell Square,	0	3	24
Pollok Street Enclosure,	0	1	20
Blythswood Drive Enclosure,	0	1	24
Wishart Street Enclosure,	0	2	16
Total,	699	2	6

APPENDIX III.

CENSUS OF VISITORS TO THE PUBLIC PARKS ON SUNDAY, 6TH AUGUST, 1893.

	No.
Glasgow Green,	78,420
Kelvingrove Park,	48,175
Queen's Park,	43,300
Alexandra Park,	15,810
Maxwell Park,	9,500
Ruchill Park,	3,790
Springburn Park,	2,097
Cathkin Braes,	2,725
Maryhill Park,	1,089
Total,	204,906

APPENDIX IV.

ESTIMATED ATTENDANCE AT THE BAND PERFORMANCES GIVEN IN THE VARIOUS PARKS AND SQUARES DURING THE SEASON OF 1894.

	No. of Performances.	Total Attendance.	Average Attendance.
Botanic Gardens,	36	87,550	2,432
Kelvingrove Park,	33	199,000	6,030
Queen's Park,	33	142,400	4,315
Glasgow Green,	32	204,000	6,375
Alexandra Park,	16	15,900	994
Phœnix Square,	15	15,000	1,000
Maxwell Park,	14	9,150	654
Springburn Park,	14	14,840	1,060
Possil Park Bandstand,	14	6,100	436
Maryhill Park,	13	3,790	292
Hutcheson Square,	13	45,800	3,523
Pollok Street Bandstand,	7	12,900	1,843
Cathkin Braes,	3	1,500	500
George Square,	2	12,450	6,225
	245	770,380	

APPENDIX V.

ESTIMATED NUMBER OF PLANTS AND BULBS BEDDED OUT IN GLASGOW GREEN, KELVINGROVE PARK, QUEEN'S PARK, ALEXANDRA PARK, MAXWELL PARK, AND OTHER OPEN SPACES, DURING THE SEASON OF 1894.

	Plants and Bulbs.
Queen's Park,	77,000
Kelvingrove Park,	60,000
Glasgow Green,	40,000
Alexandra Park,	40,000
Maxwell Park,	15,500
Public Squares, Churchyards, &c.,	16,000

APPENDIX VI.

ESTIMATED NUMBER OF SURPLUS PLANTS DISTRIBUTED TO THE PUBLIC AT THE VARIOUS PARKS AT THE CLOSE OF SEASON 1894.

Queen's Park,	8,000
Kelvingrove Park,	5,000
Glasgow Green,	1,000
Alexandra Park,	1,000
Maxwell Park,	800
	15,800

APPENDIX VII.

REPTILES, AMPHIBIANS, AND FISHES IN KELVINGROVE PARK.

REPTILES.

Viviparous Lizard, *Lacerta vivipara*, Jacq.—In the summer of 1880 a dead specimen, much decomposed, was found on the west bank of the Kelvin, opposite the Museum, among the debris on the river bank. In all probability it may have been carried down from the upper reaches of the Kelvin.

AMPHIBIANS.

Common Frog, *Rana temporaria*, L.—Occasionally found; the last one was seen on 6th May, 1894, between the Park Road and Prince of Wales' Bridges.

Common Toad, *Bufo vulgaris*, Laur.—Occasionally seen. Three were found in 1893, but none this year (1894).

Common Smooth Newt, *Molge vulgaris*, L.—Scarce. Has been found in 1876, 1877, 1879, 1880-87, 1890, 1892, and 1894.

Palmated Newt, *Molge palmata*, Schn.—Found in 1879, and one female found on the carriage drive near Kelvingrove gate in July, 1894.

FISHES.

*Perch, *Perca fluviatilis*, L.—Not common, but occasionally seen in the Kelvin up till 1881; since then rarely.

APPENDIX.

Three-Spined Stickleback, *Gasterosteus aculeatus*, L.—This species and the next three have, from time to time, been found in the Kelvin, and all are now to be found in the artificial lake.

Rough-Tailed Stickleback, *Gasterosteus trachurus*, Cuv. and Val.

Half-Armed Stickleback, *Gasterosteus semiarmatus*, Cuv. and Val.

Smooth-Tailed Stickleback, *Gasterosteus gymnurus*, Cuv.

Ten-Spined Stickleback, *Gasterosteus pungitius*, L.—Twice found at the mouth of a drain into the Kelvin near the green-houses.

Flounder, *Pleuronectes flesus*, L.—One was caught at Partick Bridge in 1880. This species has been frequently taken in the docks at the mouth of the Kelvin.

Salmon, *Salmo salar*, L.—In 1874 a few Smolt were taken in the Kelvin, but since then rarely seen; the last one in 1887.

*Trout, *Salmo trutta*, L.—Rarely seen.

Pike, *Esox lucius*, L.—Twice seen, once in 1884, and a dying one in 1886.

*Roach, *Leuciscus rutilus*, L.—Frequent.

*Minnow, *Leuciscus phoxinus*, L.—Frequent, and, like the last species, often at the mouths of surface drains into the Kelvin.

Loach, *Nemacheilus barbatula*, L.—Rare.

Eel, *Anguilla vulgaris*, Flem.—Frequent, and sometimes in the water-supply pipes; two of the latter measured 19 and 24 inches respectively.

River Lamprey, *Petromyzon fluviatilis*, L.—One was found in the Kelvin fastened to a dead Roach in 1886.

The species above marked (*) have, in addition to the following, been introduced into the artificial lake since 1886.

Common Carp, *Cyprinus carpio*, L.

Common Tench, *Tinca vulgaris*, Cuv.

www.ingramcontent.com/pod-product-compliance
Lightning Source LLC
Chambersburg PA
CBHW020912230426
43666CB00008B/1425